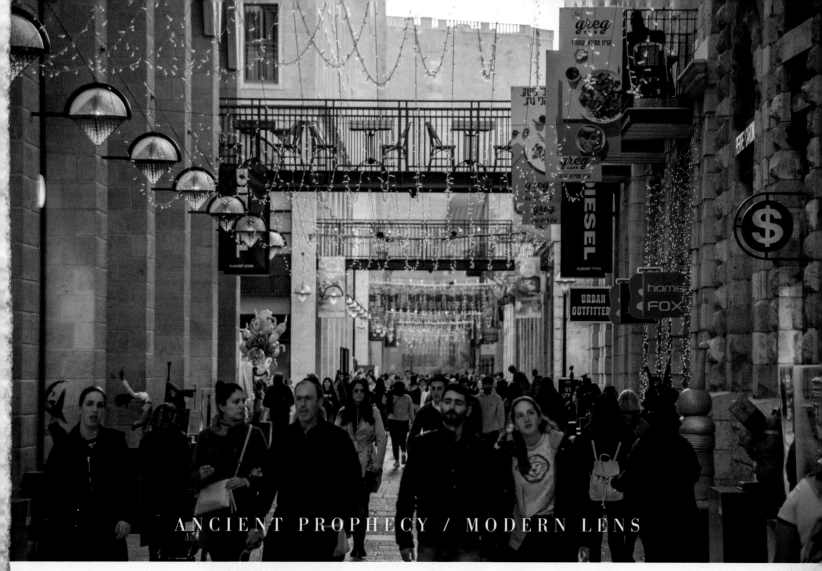

ANCIENT PROPHECY / MODERN LENS

JERUSALEM RISING

The City of Peace Reawakens

DOUG HERSHEY

Photography Edden Ram

Tyndale

Tyndale House Publishers
Carol Stream, Illinois

JERUSALEM RISING
Points of Interest

Colorful markets
of the Old City

PRESENTED TO:

Lorraine Calderwood

FROM:

Jim & Grynne-Leigh

DATE:

25 - 12 - 21

Living Expressions invites you to explore God's Word in a way
that is refreshing to your spirit and restorative to your soul.

Visit Tyndale online at tyndale.com.

Visit Doug Hershey's websites at doughershey.co and ezraadventures.com.

Visit Edden Ram's website at eddenram.com.

Design and production by Koechel Peterson and Associates, Minneapolis, Minnesota

Published in association with Yochanan Marcellino, City of Peace Media, Inc., Nashville, Tennessee. Visit cityofpeace.com.

For information about special discounts for bulk purchases, please contact Tyndale House Publishers at
csresponse@tyndale.com, or call 1-855-277-9400.

Library of Congress Cataloging-in-Publication Data is available.

ISBN 978-1-4964-5390-7

Printed in China

27   26   25   24   23   22   21
7   6   5   4   3   2   1

CONTENTS

DEDICATION

To Elijah, Josiah, Levi, and Rachel. I'm so proud of who you have become! You may not remember, but our journey began in this city with each of you being carried in my arms—Elijah was six, Josiah four, Levi two, and Rachel six weeks. It's also where my name—"Abba"—first stuck, thanks to Jerusalem's playgrounds. Now as you enter adulthood, may your hearts always be drawn to return to our beginning and to where our heavenly Abba has chosen to live—Jerusalem. I'll meet you there! ~ *Abba*

SPECIAL THANKS

Thank you to the many around the world who have enjoyed *Israel Rising* and kicked off the Ancient Prophecy/Modern Lens series, which provides a visual exploration of Ancient Prophecy, captured through a Modern Lens.

Edden, your insistence to "get it right," arguing in Hebrew and sneaking us into unlikely places while trekking fourteen kilometers a day in Jerusalem, made this five-day shoot unforgettable! Truly amazing work! My beloved Rachel, what a joy for us to be together on these shoots! Our secret cameos are forever engraved in these pages—*shhh . . .* 😉. My agent, Yochanan Marcellino, I'm grateful for your undying drive for excellence and have learned to trust your solid counsel. I'm blessed to be on this "Rising" road with you.

John Peterson, David Koechel, Sara Marino, and Jon Godfredson (Koechel Peterson and Associates), thank you for all your hard work behind the scenes and for being the very best designers in the business. Steve Zacharius/Kensington Publishing, thank you for seeing the vision of this series and allowing it to grow. Doug Knox, Becky Brandvik, and Jeff Rustemeyer at Tyndale House Publishers, thanks for embracing the Ancient Prophecy/Modern Lens vision, and Becky, thank you for directing every detail of this unique and timely series and for your tireless dedication to bringing *Jerusalem Rising* to fruition. Anisa Baker, having an editor who has been to Jerusalem more than once made this process so smooth for me!

Thank you, Kevin Jessip of Global Strategic Alliance (GSA)/The Return, for your generous support and personal introductions; Rabbi Yehudah Glick, for inspiring millions—myself included—with your amazing work regarding the Temple Mount, and for such a powerful and meaningful foreword; Rabbi Jonathan Cahn, for partnering our like-minded visions of this city and providing your heart-stirring insight in the introduction section of this work; and Lynn McCain, McCain & Co. PR, for being a consistent and faithful driver from the beginning with *Israel Rising*.

Joshua Aaron and the Music House, thanks for my Galilean home away from home, an amazingly creative place to write, and for the honor of allowing me to be the first! Thanks to Duby Tal/Albatross Aerial Photography for the stunning cover shot of the Old City. Sam Interrante, love those headshots. Thanks to Todd Bolen/BiblePlaces.com and the Library of Congress Prints and Photographs Division for permission to use the American Colony (copyright © American Colony) and the Eric Matson (copyright © Eric Matson) black-and-white photo collections. Thanks to Julia Skinner for permission to use those beautiful shots from the 1850s (FrancisFrith.com, copyright © The Francis Frith Collection) and the beautiful IAA archival photo (copyright © Courtesy of the Israel Antiquities Authority). Thanks also to Sam Noerr/Gyroscope Graphics and Mark Maxwell for your legal counsel.

*When the L*ORD* brought back the captive ones of Zion,*
we were like those who dream."

Psalm 126:1, NASB

Thank you, Lord, for the honor of sharing the changes in your city and helping to restore "the captive ones," as the psalmist promised. Many times I do feel like I'm in a dream when you exchange my own tears for joy as you bring me back to Zion again and again. For all my days, thank you.

FOREWORD

by Rabbi Yehudah Glick, former member of the Israeli Knesset

For centuries, historians around the world have pondered a mysterious secret. Though archaeologists have unearthed remnants of dozens of remarkable cultures and civilizations, of massive and complex empires of the ancient Near East—the Babylonians, ancient Egyptians, Canaanites, Akkadians, Sumerians, Hurrians, and many, many more—all but one have disappeared and become lost to history as distinctive entities. Only the People of Israel, of the smallest nations from the Fertile Crescent, have survived against all odds. They not only survived the destruction of their capital and death of their State in spite of all vicissitudes, but also brought to the world a legacy which serves until current times as the foundation of the major religions of the Western world—Judaism, Christianity, and Islam. What is the secret of this unique People?

Anyone who has opened The Book—the Hebrew Bible—is aware of the answer to this question. The secret is the Covenant the Lord made with the Patriarch Abraham. God promised him progeny, blessing, and land and assigned him a mission: to be the source of Divine blessing to all the families of the world.

Later in history, Hashem chose King David to lead the royal family. David swore not to give sleep to his eyes nor slumber to his eyelids until finding a place for the Lord's Divine Presence to dwell. Finally, Hashem pronounced the city of Jerusalem as the capital of His Kingdom, the desire of His habitation.

These blessings and assignments are the essence of the words of the prophets, who speak of all nations streaming to Jerusalem, striving to ascend the Lord's mount to listen to the teachings of His ways and go in His paths, for out of Zion shall the Torah come forth, and the word of the Lord from Jerusalem (Isaiah 2:3).

The secret of the survival of the People of Israel is a minor one compared to the phenomenon of their return in the redemption process we have been witnessing in past decades. The city of Jerusalem has been awaiting the return home of her People and is flourishing like never before. The past is reawakening, and the nations are pouring into the City of God to receive the promised blessings.

For the past two decades, I have been privileged to guide thousands of tourists from all over the world around the State of Israel, but mainly to Jerusalem. I always imagine—to myself and out loud with my tourists—the reactions of the listeners when they heard the prophet Isaiah talking about Jerusalem becoming a House of Prayer for all nations—nations who would fill the streets of the city. I remind myself that in his time the other nations were idol worshipers and the city of Jerusalem a tiny village of a few hundred acres. I recall that this was an era with no trains, buses, airplanes, or any other serious means of transportation. How did Isaiah dare think of such an illusion, that nations worldwide would be interested in this neglected city? How would people manage to get there?

We all stand astonished and privileged to live in these days when the words of the prophets are coming alive from the pages of The Book, materializing and becoming a reality. We see how Jerusalem is standing up to her name—the City of Shalom. (This is also why I gave the organization I established the name "Shalom Jerusalem.")

Many mistakenly think the word *shalom* means "peace." Actually, shalom is something much greater. It originates from the word *shalem*, meaning in Hebrew "complete, comprehensive." Shalom refers to inclusiveness, diversity. In our tradition, it is also God's name—Harmony. It reflects the legacy of the Bible's battle against separate gods. It speaks up as a city calling out to all nations to come serve the Lord on Zion, His chosen mountain, and to unite in spite of differences. One world, One God.

Today, reviewing this wonderful book by Doug Hershey identifying Jerusalem's venues and comparing the magnificent photography of what was and what is, my eyes are filled with tears. The monumental buildings are coming to life; the faces of men, women, and children are crying out with joy coming from deep in their souls. The city is lively. Millions of prayers from generation to generation—*"Next year in Jerusalem"*—are being fulfilled in ways no one could have ever dreamt.

The hands of the God of history are more evident than ever before.

Rabbi Yehudah Glick,
Shalom Jerusalem Foundation
Jerusalem, February 2021

Author Doug Hershey and Photographer Edden Ram, from the roof of the King David Hotel

INTRODUCTION

by Jonathan Cahn, author and leader of Hope of the World Ministries/Beth Israel–Jerusalem Center

The LORD says this: "I will return to Zion and dwell in the midst of Jerusalem. Then Jerusalem will be called the City of Truth, and the mountain of the LORD of armies will be called the Holy Mountain." The LORD of armies says this: "Old men and old women will again sit in the public squares of Jerusalem, each person with his staff in his hand because of age. And the public squares of the city will be filled with boys and girls playing in its squares."

ZECHARIAH 8:3-5, NASB

Yerushalayim, Jerusalem—the City of cities, the habitation of God's presence and glory, the city of Messiah and His salvation, and the epicenter of biblical prophecy. Jerusalem—what was, what is, and what is yet to come.

Without Jerusalem, the purposes of God cannot come to pass. Upon this unlikely mountaintop city of rocks, resting between pastureland on one side and desert on the other, rests the fate of the world, of human history, and of the cosmos itself.

For most of the past two thousand years, Jerusalem was a neglected ruin of a city—overlooked, forgotten, languishing. And yet in the ancient prophecy of Zechariah, God promises He will remember His city and return to it. It will rise from its tomb and be filled again with old men and women, boys and girls playing in its squares. And for most of the past two thousand years, such words appeared the stuff of fantasy, an impossible dream.

Yet after nearly two thousand years and against all odds, the words of the prophets were fulfilled as the hand of God gathered His scattered people back to their ancient homeland. But it could not be complete until the Jewish people returned to their Holy City, Jerusalem. And so in June of 1967, as Israeli soldiers entered the gates of the Temple Mount, the other ancient prophecies were fulfilled: The Jewish people had returned to Jerusalem.

It was only the beginning of the miracle. What followed was nothing short of a prophetic resurrection. It is for this reason that when I lead tours to the land of Israel, I always make sure to stop inside the Old City and there recite the prophecy of Zechariah 8, of the children playing in the city's squares. Yet it has never happened that I've read those words and the tourists have seen, in living color, Jewish children playing in the squares—prophecy fulfilled in flesh and blood.

And that is why Doug Hershey's *Jerusalem Rising* is so powerful. It is a witness in graphic imagery to the reality of God's existence, the truth of His Word, the record of His hand in the affairs of human history, the faithfulness of His promises, and His love and mercy toward His ancient people. The images in the book are not matters of opinion or feeling but are the immutable stones that cry out, *"God is real, and His love endures forever."*

They not only cry out but also prophesy, *"Messiah is coming again"*—for the return of the Jewish people to Jerusalem is the prophetic prerequisite for Messiah's return, on the day they will cry out, *"Baruch haba b'Shem Adonai"*—"Blessed is He who comes in the Name of the Lord."

May this book strengthen and encourage all who put their hope in Him, the Messiah—the Light of the World, the Hope of Israel, and the King of Jerusalem.

Jonathan Cahn

> " *After all, I think Jerusalem is part of . . .*
> *the world's heritage.* "
> *King Hussein of Jordan*

Revisiting the spot where I stood on the Mount of Olives years ago

> " *The view of Jerusalem is the history of the world; it*
> *is more, it is the history of earth and of heaven.* "
> *Benjamin Disraeli, nineteenth-century British prime minister,*
> *Tancred*, vol. 1 (New York: M. Walter Dunne, 1904), 23–24

PREFACE

On a fall day during Sukkot (the Feast of Tabernacles), I was standing on the Mount of Olives with a bus group of Christians and Jews, overlooking the Old City from one of the most iconic spots in Jerusalem. The sun was warm against the cool autumn breeze, the sky a vibrant blue, with white, wispy clouds blowing in directional chaos. For the few minutes we had there among the hustle and bustle, it seemed I was all alone.

As my eyes accepted the famed view and my heart began to settle, what impacted me the most were the clouds overhead. They looked so familiar, like the ones I used to see over my childhood home. I had an overwhelming revelation that the mysterious, faraway city of Jerusalem I had read about as a kid was a tangible location with real people, problems, and events—and with real promises—all covered in white, puffy clouds! This place, the stories, its destiny . . . just like those clouds, they were as inexplicably real and familiar as my life on the other side of the world.

More than twenty years later, I don't remember much about my ten-day trip, aside from that brief encounter with the clouds. It was when I suddenly understood that my life—somehow, some way—would be interwoven with this city and region. Even if it took another twenty to thirty years, I knew then that Jerusalem was where I belonged and needed to go back to. As a prominent rabbi would later tell me, "The pull of Jerusalem is like gravity—you can't escape it." Since that life-changing moment, I've realized my story is not unique, both throughout history and in our current day. What in the human heart feels such an unexplainable pull toward this city? Across the ages, people of different backgrounds, cultures, and religions have all sensed it and responded.

Jerusalem is unique among all cities on earth; no other city changes people so dramatically upon their first visit. No other city's future has been foretold, from its destruction to its rebirth to its prophesied rise back to center stage in the theater of history. Even through the centuries of its desolation, it has been prayed for, sought after, fought against, and wept over. Yet it wasn't until the return of the Jewish people, who had made it their capital, that Jerusalem truly began to revive. This stunning revival is still occurring today, as you will soon see. And while it is happening, hearts are still being drawn to Jerusalem—perhaps even your own.

Ironically, Jerusalem—the "City of Peace," as its name means in Hebrew—has been attacked or besieged more than seventy times, has changed hands more than forty times, and was completely destroyed at least twice. As historian Simon Montefiore writes, Jerusalem is *the desire and prize of empires, yet of no strategic value* (Simon Sebag Montefiore, *Jerusalem: The Biography* [New York: Alfred A. Knopf, 2011], xxi). Historically it was a small mountainous city away from any viable trade route, with only an average water source and no coastal access or natural resources. There is no earthly reason why anyone would want to control Jerusalem. Yet a spiritual reason is another matter.

"*Jerusalem is a witness, an echo of eternity. Stand still and listen.*"
A. J. Heschel, twentieth-century Polish-born American rabbi and Jewish theologian,
from "An Echo of Eternity," quoted in *I Asked for Wonder* (New York: Crossroad, 1984), 116

> *"You're shaking. . . . So am I. It's because of Jerusalem, isn't it? One doesn't go to Jerusalem, one returns to it. That's one of its mysteries."*
>
> Elie Wiesel, renowned writer, Nobel Prize recipient, and Holocaust survivor,
> *A Beggar in Jerusalem* (New York: Random House, 1970), 186

Jerusalem's connection to the God of the Bible is undeniable. Specifically, he said it is the only city where he has chosen to dwell: "For the LORD has chosen Zion, he has desired it for his dwelling, saying, 'This is my resting place for ever and ever'" (Psalm 132:13-14). This alone sets it apart from any other place on the planet. The numerous ancient prophecies that surround the destruction and future revival of Jerusalem are remarkably unique, one of which we will look at in the pages ahead. For centuries, devout men and women have been looking for and praying toward that glorious end, a fact which is also unrivaled with any other city.

In the second century, one such account of this hope was written about Rabbi Akiva, as recorded in the Talmud many years later:

Once [Rabbi Akiva and three fellow Sages] were coming up to Jerusalem. When they reached Mount Scopus, they rent their garments. When they came to the Temple Mount they saw a fox emerging from the Holy of Holies, and they started to weep. But Rabbi Akiva smiled. His companions said to him, "Why are you smiling?" He replied, "Why are you weeping?" They said, "A place about which it is written: A stranger who comes close shall be put to death (Numbers 1:51), and now foxes are walking about there—should we not weep?" "That is why I am smiling," Rabbi Akiva replied, reminding them that the Prophets had foretold both the destruction of Jerusalem and its restoration. "Now that the prophecy of its desolation has been fulfilled," he said, "I know that its restoration will also come to pass"

(Talmud, Makkot 24b, quoted in Jack Friedman, *The Jerusalem Book of Quotations: A 3,000-Year Perspective* [Jerusalem: Gefen, 2007], 22).

It was while working in and flying over Jerusalem during photo shoots for *Israel Rising*, the first book in the Ancient Prophecy/Modern Lens series, that I knew I needed to return to focus only on this city and the mystique it carries. Since then, a quote from Shmuel Yosef Agnon has stirred my heart and become my prayer: *"I returned to Jerusalem, and it is by virtue of Jerusalem that I have written all that God has put into my heart and into my pen"* ("Shmuel Agnon Banquet Speech," nobelprize.org). I have prayed the same will be true of this project.

In the pages ahead, you'll read a compelling ancient prophecy. Written nearly 2,600 years ago, parts of it defy logic and fly in the face of the last two millennia of human history. Given traditional conflicts, the prophecy's predictions seem unlikely or even impossible. They foretell the revival of the city—the restoration of life and honoring of a Jewish culture that, until the Six-Day War of 1967, seemed to be a distant, idealistic dream. Yet within our lifetimes, much of it has begun to unfold in an unprecedented way.

The awe-inspiring photography in this book contains visual treasures that few have ever seen. I obtained some of the oldest photos ever taken of Jerusalem—from the 1840s to 1860s—for the purpose of reshooting them as accurately as possible, showing the dramatic changes that have occurred in such a short amount of time. For many of these photos, we found the "X" that marked the spot on

which these early adventurous photographers stood. In cases where an older style of photography was used, the locations were particularly difficult to find. But once we understood a key aspect of how those photos were recently presented, we identified the correct angle and retook the shots, perhaps for the first time in 175 years.

I've also included many photos from the American Colony Collection (ACC) that were not in my previous book, *Israel Rising*. Whenever possible, priority was given to the early and rare photos, as few have seen pictures of Jerusalem from this era, let alone compared them to photos taken from those exact angles today. Many times, shooting from the exact angle was not possible due to the growth of vegetation, buildings, and population . . . and yet these changes are precisely what were prophesied. The results are astounding.

You'll also read short vignettes of my "Personal Encounters"—accounts of people I got to know while on the photo shoot, including my Israeli photographer, Edden Ram. Born in America but raised in Israel, Edden is a talented and adventurous travel photographer in his own right. He not only captured some of the most amazing photography of Jerusalem that I've ever seen, but also the essence of the Israeli heart and the spirit of these early photos. In our drive to find "*the* spot" for each photo, we climbed more walls and fences; ignored, schmoozed, or argued with more security guards; and quietly got in and out of more sticky areas than I will admit to. He was perfect for this project.

Finally, you'll read quotes revealing how Jerusalem has motivated both soul-stirring devotion and warmongering claims, capturing the desires of Jews, Christians, and Muslims for the last two thousand years. From Christopher Columbus's request that profits from his exploration be used to recover Jerusalem to Turkish President Recep Tayyip Erdoğan's statement claiming his country has a stake in Jerusalem, it's undeniable that even in Jerusalem's desolation, this city has continued to seize hearts and blur the lines between the impassioned, the devout, and the obsessed. There is a reason why.

At the end of the book, the decision will be yours to make: Is this all just a historical coincidence, or is the ancient prophecy coming to pass? Like Rabbi Akiva's wisdom demonstrates, if the destruction has come to pass and restoration is beginning, perhaps we can expect the rest to unfold as well. As the history of Jerusalem has already demonstrated from the beginning, time will tell.

It is my distinct honor to welcome you home to a unique perspective of Jerusalem—the center of the earth!

Doug Hershey

> *Jerusalem of gold, and of bronze and of light,*
> *behold I am a violin for all of your songs"*
>
> Naomi Shemer, "Jerusalem of Gold"

WHY JERUSALEM?

One of the most ancient and historical cities in the world, Jerusalem has captured the hearts and minds of the nations for three millennia. Originally it was a small and isolated mountainous city, built on one of the smallest hills in the Judaean range at the point where the Kidron, Tyropoeon, and Hinnom valleys join. As mentioned before, the city held little strategic value positioned away from ancient trade routes. Even today, it has little, if any, natural resources and only a meager water source. At best, its location is unimpressive. Yet it has continued to find itself at the center of world plans, goals, and conflicts.

While it was more than three thousand years ago that King David made Jerusalem Israel's capital, he was not the first to capture the city. One of its early historical mentions is in the Scriptures, where the book of Judges mentions that the tribes of Judah and Benjamin both fought the Jebusites for control over the city. Yet Israel wasn't able to hold it until King David conquered and finally subdued the Jebusites, securing Jerusalem and making it his capital.

This act likely contributed to Israel's love for David. His childhood home was in Bethlehem, a mere five miles away, and as king and military leader over Israel, he could have established a comfortable capital city in his hometown. Instead, he chose to live on the front lines with his warriors, risking his own life to ensure the city remained Israel's capital. Since then it has remained on the front lines throughout history, even struggling to retain its Jewish identity. Midway through the twentieth century, Winston Churchill quipped, *"You ought to let the Jews have Jerusalem; it is they who made it famous"* (quoted in Evelyn Shuckburgh, *Descent to Suez* [New York: W. W. Norton, 1987], 251).

Yet King David was not the only one who chose Jerusalem. Around the same time, it was becoming clear that the Lord had also chosen it to be more than a mere earthly city:

> The LORD appeared to [David's son Solomon] at night and said: . . . *"I have chosen and consecrated this temple [in Jerusalem]* **so that my Name may be there forever**. *My eyes and my heart will always be there."*
>
> 2 CHRONICLES 7:12, 16, EMPHASIS ADDED

> The LORD, the God of Israel, says: . . . *"I will give one tribe to [Solomon's] son so that David my servant may always have a lamp before me in Jerusalem,* **the city where I chose to put my Name.**"
>
> 1 KINGS 11:31, 36, EMPHASIS ADDED

From the time of Moses, God said he would bring Israel to the place he had chosen for his name to dwell forever. Perhaps this was not simply symbolic or metaphorical but literal as well. In the Hebrew language, the combinations of letters that form words have meaning, and the letters themselves often represent specific words. The twenty-first letter of the Hebrew alphabet is the letter shin (ש), and in Jewish tradition, it represents the word *El Shaddai*, one of the names of God.

We find this letter in many traditional and religious settings relating to the Torah (the first five books of the Bible, written by Moses) and to God. It can be seen on mezuzahs (little boxes holding tiny scrolls of specific Scriptures, fastened to the doorposts of Jewish homes) and on phylacteries (small boxes with specific Scriptures, often worn on the arms and above the foreheads of religious Jews while praying). It's also the shape the high priests made with their hands while extending their arms to bless the people of Israel.

As you can see, the shin is a significant letter in Judaism. When looking at old aerial photos or a topographical map of Jerusalem, it's evident that the city's three valleys naturally form the crude shape of

YEAR	PERIOD	LAND NAME	EYEWITNESS ACCOUNTS OF THE LAND
UNDER FOREIGN RULE			
539–332 BC	Persian Empire, return of exiles, Second Temple	Judah/Jerusalem	Ezra; Nehemiah; Zechariah; Haggai
332–142 BC	Greek Empire	Judah/Jerusalem	1 Maccabees 1:29-39
JEWISH INDEPENDENCE			
142–63 BC	Hasmonean Dynasty	Judah/Jerusalem	1 Maccabees 14:5-12
UNDER FOREIGN RULE			
63–37 BC	Roman Empire	Judah/Jerusalem	
37–4 BC	Roman Empire/Herod	Judah/Jerusalem	
4 BC–AD 70	Roman Empire/procurators	Judah/Jerusalem	Flavius Josephus
70–136	Roman Empire/Jewish expulsion	Aelia Capitolina	Pliny the Elder
136–306	Bar Kochbah Revolt/ Roman Empire	Palestine/ Aelia Capitolina	Dio Cassius
306–614	Byzantine Empire	Palestine/Jerusalem	Helena; Paula of Bethlehem; St. Jerome
614–628	Neo-Persian/Sasanian Empire	Palestine/Jerusalem	
628–638	Byzantine Empire	Palestine/Jerusalem	Sophronius
638–1099	Multiple Muslim/Arab caliphates	Palestine/Jerusalem	Mukaddasi
1099–1291	Crusades	Palestine/Jerusalem	Nahmanides
1291–1516	Mamluk Sultanate	Palestine/Jerusalem	Niccolò of Poggibonsi
1516–1917	Ottoman Empire	Palestine/Jerusalem	Alphonse de Lamartine; Mark Twain
1917–1948	British Mandate	Palestine/Jerusalem	Rabbi Abraham Isaac Kook
1948–1967	Kingdom of Jordan	Transjordan/ Jerusalem	David Ben-Gurion; Shmuel Yosef Agnon
JEWISH INDEPENDENCE			
1967–present	Israel	Israel/Jerusalem	Yehuda Amichai

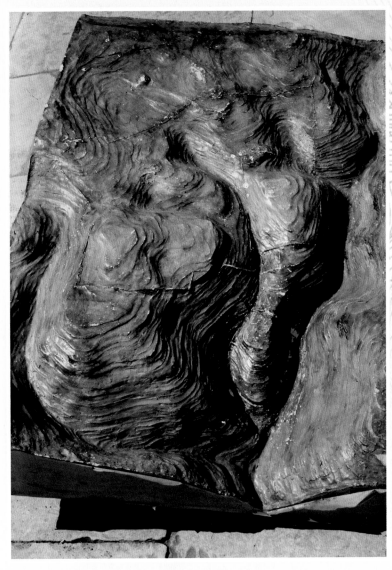

Topographical Relief Map of Jerusalem, 1934–39 (ACC—Views of the City)

North at the top. This relief map is believed to be one created by Ernest Beaufort of the American Colony community.

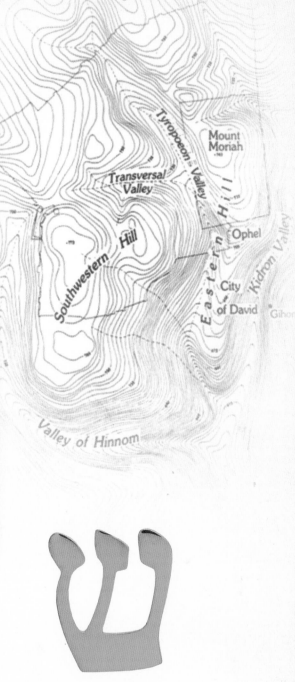

a shin, making the argument that God's name really does rest forever among Jerusalem's hills and valleys, just as the Lord spoke through the prophets.

Whether or not one recognizes the shin in the hills and valleys of Jerusalem, this isn't what makes the city unique. No other people group has the history of its capital city foretold in ancient writings. Jerusalem has no equal—from the city's conquest, destruction, and enduring desolation to its revival as a world player and prophesied seat of power for a King who will rule the earth. Furthermore, according to these

prophecies, the Creator calls the physical location of Jerusalem "home" and will personally dwell there with his people. For 1,900 years after the Romans burned the city and region—and most significantly after the decline of the Byzantine period in the fourth century—history clearly demonstrated that Jerusalem was indeed a barren wasteland. Yet dramatic changes have taken place over the last half century. Let's look at what the ancient prophecy in Zechariah 8 says about what is coming and see whether there is a connection.

THE ANCIENT PROPHECY
Zechariah 8

Zechariah lived around 2,600 years ago, at a time when the Jewish people were starting to rebuild the Temple in Jerusalem after returning from the Babylonian exile. Around 520 BC, after many years of inactivity in the work of restoration, the prophet began encouraging the people to finish the task. He also foretold that many hopeful and amazing things would happen when they were back in the Land, some of which seemed not only distant but also impossible. Yet in this portion of his prophecy, it was not Zechariah alone who was speaking to the people.

Zechariah 8

¹ The word of the LORD Almighty came to me.

² This is what the LORD Almighty says: "I am very jealous for Zion; I am burning with jealousy for her."

³ This is what the LORD says: "I will return to Zion and dwell in Jerusalem. Then Jerusalem will be called the Faithful City, and the mountain of the LORD Almighty will be called the Holy Mountain."

⁴ This is what the LORD Almighty says: "Once again men and women of ripe old age will sit in the streets of Jerusalem, each of them with cane in hand because of their age. ⁵ The city streets will be filled with boys and girls playing there."

⁶ This is what the LORD Almighty says: "It may seem marvelous to the remnant of this people at that time, but will it seem marvelous to me?" declares the LORD Almighty.

⁷ This is what the LORD Almighty says: "I will save my people from the countries of the east and the west. ⁸ I will bring them back to live in Jerusalem; they will be my people, and I will be faithful and righteous to them as their God."

⁹ This is what the LORD Almighty says: "Now hear these words, 'Let your hands be strong so that the temple may be built.' This is also what the prophets said who were present when the foundation was laid for the house of the LORD Almighty. ¹⁰ Before that time there were no wages for people or hire for animals. No one could go about their business safely because of their enemies, since I had turned everyone against their neighbor. ¹¹ But now I will not deal with the remnant of this people as I did in the past," declares the LORD Almighty.

¹² "The seed will grow well, the vine will yield its fruit, the ground will produce its crops, and the heavens will drop their dew. I will give all these things as an inheritance to the remnant of this people. ¹³ Just as you, Judah and Israel, have been a curse among the

nations, so I will save you, and you will be a blessing. Do not be afraid, but let your hands be strong."

14 This is what the LORD Almighty says: "Just as I had determined to bring disaster on you and showed no pity when your ancestors angered me," says the LORD Almighty, 15 "so now I have determined to do good again to Jerusalem and Judah. Do not be afraid. 16 These are the things you are to do: Speak the truth to each other, and render true and sound judgment in your courts; 17 do not plot evil against each other, and do not love to swear falsely. I hate all this," declares the LORD.

18 The word of the LORD Almighty came to me.

19 This is what the LORD Almighty says: "The fasts of the fourth, fifth, seventh and tenth months will become joyful and glad occasions and happy festivals for Judah. Therefore love truth and peace."

20 This is what the LORD Almighty says: "Many peoples and the inhabitants of many cities will yet come, 21 and the inhabitants of one city will go to another and say, 'Let us go at once to entreat the LORD and seek the LORD Almighty. I myself am going.' 22 And many peoples and powerful nations will come to Jerusalem to seek the LORD Almighty and to entreat him."

23 This is what the LORD Almighty says: "In those days ten people from all languages and nations will take firm hold of one Jew by the hem of his robe and say, 'Let us go with you, because we have heard that God is with you.'"

While there is much to say about these words, let's look at three aspects that are directly related to promises to the city and the people of Jerusalem. First, the most noticeable theme centers on exactly who is speaking (the Lord) and what his intentions are. Second, there are specific promises relating to the revival of the life, land, and population of Jerusalem. And third, there are some stunning promises that the city, as well as the people, will have honor and prominence.

(1) THE LORD'S RETURN TO JERUSALEM

Zechariah 8 starts with God telling us he is jealous for Zion—another name for Jerusalem—and that he wants to live there. It is hard to get past this dramatic and clear statement. Notice that God is not speaking to the prophet, asking him to tell anyone who would listen. Rather, he is speaking directly to the people about his plans and intentions. Fourteen different times, we are told who the speaker is with repeated phrases like *"the LORD Almighty says," "declares the LORD,"* and *"says the LORD."* Other places in Zechariah's writings communicate his personal visions and experiences where God is talking to him. Since that's not the case here, there can be no mistaking that in this prophecy, God himself is speaking to the audience.

Notice that the Lord said he would return to Jerusalem, not plan for a first-time visit: *"I will return to Zion and dwell in Jerusalem"* (v. 3). He had already chosen it and had dwelt in Jerusalem before, during the time of David and Solomon, and here he announces he will come back because he desires to. Yet he is planning to return not to an empty and desolate city but to one filled with people he will regather from the nations. There is only one city on earth where the Creator has chosen to dwell and call home: Jerusalem.

(2) THE COMING RESTORATION

Zechariah's prophecy was written at the time when a remnant of Jewish exiles were returning to a destroyed and desolate land, resettling Jerusalem and the surrounding areas. The gates had been destroyed by fire, and Jerusalem was still in ruins from its invaders. Furthermore, they had new enemies who were watching. Yet these hopeful promises were spoken: *This is what the LORD Almighty says: 'Once again men and women of ripe old age will sit in the streets of Jerusalem, each of them with cane in hand because of their age. The city streets will be filled with boys and girls playing there'* (vv. 4-5).

These verses speak of a time of peace and security in the city. The most vulnerable of the population, the elderly and the children, will safely enjoy the streets of Jerusalem. Since the time of Zechariah and until recently, this has rarely been the case, although there has almost always been a Jewish presence in Jerusalem. From the pressure and attacks of surrounding nations during the return from Babylonian exile, to brutal Roman conquests more than two thousand years ago, to Muslim bandits who started roaming the Land in the seventh century, to the devastation of Crusaders' swords in the Middle Ages, to oppressive Ottoman taxation and the Jordanian destruction of Jewish homes and

synagogues in the Old City between 1948 and 1967 . . . peace and security have not prevailed in Jerusalem.

When Jerusalem's inhabitants were returning around the time of this prophecy, they were coming only from Babylon in the east. But in verses 7-8, God says he will save them from countries in the east *and* the west: *"This is what the LORD Almighty says: 'I will save my people from the countries of the east and the west. I will bring them back to live in Jerusalem; they will be my people, and I will be faithful and righteous to them as their God.'"* Geographically, west of Jerusalem is the vast Mediterranean Sea, not a nation with people, making this statement hard to understand for Jews at that time.

As the exiles came back, they rebuilt homes and farming communities. While they experienced a brief period of independent Jewish life and fruitfulness during the Hasmonean Kingdom in 142–63 BC, it didn't last long. According to first-century Jewish historian Flavius Josephus in his book *The Wars of the Jews*, by the time the Romans destroyed the Temple in AD 70, they had cut down trees for 90 furlongs (18.1 kilometers, or 11.25 miles) in every direction from Jerusalem. He stated that a traveler who had seen Jerusalem before would not have recognized it afterward (*The Wars of the Jews*, book 6, chap. 1 in *Complete Works of Josephus*, vol. 4 [New York: Bigelow, Brown, 1800], 272).

Most historians agree that during the fall of the Byzantine Empire, the city continued to decline, with the land suffering its greatest desolation under Ottoman rule, from 1517–1917. Their taxation of the trees and building of the railway system decimated entire forests, destroyed desert ecosystems, changed weather patterns, and eroded topsoil and ancient farming terraces, turning much of the country into either a desert or swampland. And yet in verse 12, God promises, *"The seed will grow well, the vine will yield its fruit, the ground will produce its crops, and the heavens will drop their dew. I will give all these things as an inheritance to the remnant of this people."*

(3) A PROMISE OF HONOR AND PROMINENCE

God's message in verses 20-22 must have seemed laughable: *"This is what the LORD Almighty says: 'Many peoples and the inhabitants of many cities will yet come, and the inhabitants of one city will go to another and say, "Let us go at once to entreat the LORD and seek the LORD Almighty. I myself am going." And many peoples and powerful nations will come to Jerusalem to seek the LORD Almighty and to entreat him.'"*

Not just people from other cities but also "powerful nations" will come to seek the Lord's favor in Jerusalem? At the time Zechariah was speaking, Jerusalem essentially had no defensive wall around it, and the people had left the meager Temple unfinished and unsupported. The surrounding nations were unhappy the Jews were back, and they caused trouble during the rebuilding process. Yet the prophetic word was that many prominent nations would come to seek the favor of the God of Israel in Jerusalem.

If people and powerful nations coming to Jerusalem seemed far-fetched, the prophecy in verse 23 must have been all the more so: *"This is what the LORD Almighty says: 'In those days ten people from all languages and nations will take firm hold of one Jew by the hem of his robe and say, "Let us go with you, because we have heard that God is with you."'"* In biblical Hebrew, the corner of a garment is called "kanaph." According to Numbers 15:38, Israel was to make and attach "tsitsit," or tassels, to the corners ("kanaphay") of their clothes. These tassels were to be a reminder of the Torah and God's commands to walk in his ways and not their own (v. 39). What is being suggested here isn't just that the nations will come to Jerusalem to seek the Lord for favor; it's also that the nations will grab hold of Torah standards, recognize the place and favor of the Jewish people as chosen by God, and seek to learn from them. It reflects not an outward diplomatic visit but a desire to connect with the Jewish people and live in ways that honor them.

When the sparse number of former exiles began rebuilding Jerusalem from the ashes, the items prophesied in Zechariah 8 seemed utterly fantastical: God himself will return to Jerusalem, he will regather the Jewish people from all the nations, they will live in security and peace in Jerusalem, and the nations will come not only to seek the Lord's favor in Jerusalem but also to honor and join with the Jewish people. Yet if these statements were to tangibly and literally come to pass, they knew that only God could have spoken this message and only he could take credit for it.

Throughout the centuries since these words were spoken, people from all over the world have yearned with an inexplicable fascination for this city, spurring many of them to embark on the adventure of a lifetime.

THE FIRST PHOTOGRAPHERS IN JERUSALEM

Today Jerusalem is a popular tourist destination with a growing population and an exciting international culture. Yet historical eyewitness accounts from travelers like Mark Twain tell us that Jerusalem was once a quiet, dilapidated, and empty wasteland. After spending some time in the city in 1867, Mark Twain famously wrote, *"Jerusalem is mournful, and dreary, and lifeless. I would not desire to live here"* (Mark Twain, *The Innocents Abroad* [Hartford, CT: American Publishing, 1869], 560). Upon his departure, he lamented, *"Renowned Jerusalem itself, the stateliest name in history, has lost all its ancient grandeur, and is become a pauper village; the riches of Solomon are no longer there to compel the admiration of visiting Oriental queens"* (607). It was as if any romantic notions he had of this profound, ancient biblical city were quickly overtaken by the reality of desolation that could be seen, smelled, and tasted at every turn. By the time he boarded his ship in Jaffa, he seemed eager to leave.

At least twenty-five years before Twain first shared his bleak descriptions of Jerusalem, entrepreneurial explorers embarked upon the Holy Land to document it using daguerreotype, the first revolutionary form of photography. It used a chemical reaction on a light-sensitive, silver-coated copper plate, coupled with mercury vapors and iodine, to make the process of capturing true images much faster and more mobile. Due to their commitment and artistic passion, we can see for ourselves the work and travels of these early photographers, the most notable being Joseph-Philibert Girault de Prangey. Soon pioneers like Francis Frith used even faster and easier processes in the 1860s, producing far better images. Thanks to their enduring struggles, we can see exactly what Mark Twain wrote about, as well as the state of Jerusalem twenty-five years before his arrival.

JOSEPH-PHILIBERT GIRAULT DE PRANGEY, 1842–44

Perhaps the most unlikely of these explorers, Joseph-Philibert Girault de Prangey (1804–92), has become for me an exciting and unsuspecting hero of this photo project. He was a Paris-trained painter at heart with a love for architecture and landscape. Ironically, his painting roots may have unintentionally credited him with taking Jerusalem's oldest photographs. He learned daguerreotype photography in 1841, possibly from its creator, when Louis Daguerre himself publicly demonstrated his state-of-the-art process.

Soon afterward, adventure photographers flooded the Middle East, hoping to capture the region in more accurate images that could be made available to the public. Girault de Prangey shared this excitement, traveling to Italy, Greece, and the Middle East during the early 1840s. Toward the end of his time in Jerusalem, he wrote in a letter home, *"After spending 55 days in the holy city and its environs . . . I am sure you can share*

my natural delight in fulfilling a dream cherished since childhood. . . . How happy I am to realize that in a few months I will be able to share them with you as they are, as I bear with me their precious and unquestionably faithful trace that cannot be diminished by time or distance" (quoted in Karen Chernick, "The Earliest Surviving Photographs of Jerusalem Live On in Historic Exhibit," *Jewish Standard*, February 12, 2019, jewishstandard. timesofisrael.com). Even for this French photographer, we can sense his childlike attraction to Jerusalem. Now he is a part of Jerusalem's history.

Upon returning home to France, Girault de Prangey published lithographs of watercolor paintings and ink-pen drawings that he made from his more than nine hundred daguerreotypes, while carefully storing the actual photoplates in wooden boxes. This fact alone may be why we know of him now. Many adventure-seeking photographers explored the Middle East before

Tower of David (Citadel)

The image on the left is Girault de Prangey's daguerreotype; the image on the right is the actual view in 1844.

While the current walls and tower date to the sixteenth century, this location near the Jaffa Gate has been significant since at least the Hasmonean Kingdom more than two thousand years ago, when a defensive wall and towers stood at the site. Remains of a wall dating back to King Hezekiah's reign during the First Temple period were also found. See today's comparison on page 67.

Girault de Prangey arrived, yet no known original works of his predecessors exist.

While it is said that he reportedly enjoyed showing his photographic plates to private guests, Girault de Prangey never exhibited his daguerreotypes publicly, and they were soon forgotten. It wasn't until the 1920s, about thirty years after his death, that the new owner of his run-down estate discovered these treasures in their old wooden crates. Yet the world didn't catch its first glimpse until 2003, eighty years later, when several select pieces were auctioned, with one selling for more than $900,000.

One hundred and sixty years after capturing his photos of Jerusalem, word was finally getting out regarding Girault de Prangey's photography. The Smithsonian Institution began to digitize his work and shared it online with the world in 2014, yet with one misunderstood detail. The daguerreotype plates were correctly published as they are, a perfect mirror image of the subject matter, but to the viewer, the pictures reversed the real-life perspective. Aside from local historical guides in Jerusalem understanding this fact, it

has gone largely unnoticed until now.

Ironically, in *Israel Rising*, I also published a couple of Girault de Prangey's reversed images. Before realizing this quandary in my research for this book, I would stare at one of his photos—such as *Dome of the Rock*—yet still be lost. I knew Jerusalem's backstreets and the Old City's hidden gems, but I still couldn't place the angles his shots were taken from. Hidden in plain sight, it wasn't until we reversed the images, at the prodding of a friend, that I fully recognized the true view. At that point, I knew exactly where they had been taken and where to go to enable my team to reshoot them. It is my

honor to share with you, possibly for the first time ever, these true angles and the then-now comparisons with his work, spanning more than 175 years. The results and obvious transformations are astounding and truly speak to how this city has come back from the ashes.

In these featured photographs from 1844, the image on the left reflects the actual daguerreotype plates and how they were first published. The image on the right shows the true views that one would see at these locations, which you'll find re-created throughout this book.

Dome of the Rock

The image on the left is Girault de Prangey's daguerreotype;
the image on the right is the actual view in 1844.

One of the more well-known shrines in Jerusalem, the Dome of the Rock, was built in the late seventh century, within the first sixty years of the founding of Islam. Ironically, the structure was originally based on Byzantine church and palace construction. It is situated over what many consider to be a rock called the Foundation Stone, where according to Jewish tradition, God created Adam, Abraham almost sacrificed Isaac, and the First and Second Temples stood. See today's comparison on page 135.

Village of Silwan

*The image on the left is Girault de Prangey's daguerreotype photo;
the image on the right is the actual view in 1844.*

Located across the Kidron Valley from the ancient City of David and known today as Silwan, this village dates back to biblical times. The area has often been referred to as the "Hill of Corruption" since it's here that King Solomon built a shrine to the foreign gods of his wives (1 Kings 11:7-8; 2 Kings 23:13); idols from the time of Solomon have even been found at this site. Prestigious biblical tombs are also located on this hillside, dating to the same era. See today's comparison on page 175.

Jerusalem from Mount Scopus

The top photo is Girault de Prangey's daguerreotype; the bottom photo is the actual view in 1844.

One of the most revealing shots from this early time period shows the size and dimensions of Jerusalem in 1844. The same year, an Ottoman Empire census recorded over fifteen thousand people living in Jerusalem, with more than seven thousand inhabitants being Jewish. This photo was taken from Mount Scopus, where the primary Roman command post under Titus was located during the siege of Jerusalem and the Temple's destruction in AD 70. Today it is where Hebrew University stands. See today's comparison on pages 186–87.

Lions' Gate

The Lions' Gate, on the eastern side of the Old City. The image on the left is
Girault de Prangey's daguerreotype; the image on the right is the actual view in 1844.

Jacob's prophecy in Genesis 49:9-10 connected the tribe of Judah with the symbol of a lion and Israel's future monarchy. Because the nation's kings ruled from Jerusalem, Israel's capital, the lion became a vital part of the city's identity and history. Ironically and according to legend, in the early sixteenth century the Ottoman sultan Selim had plans to destroy Jerusalem until he dreamed that lions were eating him for doing so. After promising to protect the city with a wall, he was saved. The next sultan, Süleyman the Magnificent, rebuilt the walls around 1538 and added the protective lions, or leopards, to the gate. See today's comparison on page 83.

Temple Mount

The top photo is Girault de Prangey's daguerreotype; the bottom photo is the actual view in 1844.

This rarely seen angle of the Temple Mount, taken from a second story window in the Old City, shows a desolate landscape. The Mount of Olives, seen in the background, lies barren, while the foreground is unkempt and the buildings stand forgotten in disrepair. With only about fifteen thousand people in the city at the time, the famed Temple Mount seemed insignificant. See today's comparison, along with the Personal Encounters story of how we got the shot, on pages 138–39.

Pool of Hezekiah

*This reservoir, believed to be built by King Hezekiah,
contained nearly three million gallons at capacity.
It continued to hold water up to recent times.*

FRANCIS FRITH, 1857–60

By 1856, Francis Frith had sold his holdings in a successful grocery store and printing business and started a photography studio near London. Soon he felt sufficiently competent to take the cumbersome equipment required for his first tour of Egypt, and as soon as 1857 he embarked on his second trip, adding Palestine and Syria to his itinerary.

Throughout Frith's travels, the heat and strong light drove him to develop his photographic plates in temples, caves, and tombs. In his book *Camera: A History of Photography*, Todd Gustavson states that Frith's *"pictures of the Sphinx, the pyramids, and other scenes from Egypt and the Holy Land made him a legend"* ([New York: Sterling Signature, 2012], 38). Despite Frith's drive for adventure, it seems his impressions of Jerusalem weren't much different from Mark Twain's, who visited ten years later. Frith described it as a *"greenly city . . . crowned but fearfully desolate. Holy and beautiful but terribly debased and defiled"* (Ely Schiller, ed., *The First Photographs of Jerusalem and the Holy Land* [Jerusalem: Ariel, 1980], 233).

Frith is considered to be one of the first photographers to cover the Holy Land in its entirety. Due to his entrepreneurial mindset, he is also recognized as one of the first photographers to sell landscape photography as a successful retailer. People soon began buying his work, and they are still doing so today. In 1858, the *London Times* marveled at this new photographic medium Frith was helping to pioneer. They said his works *"carry us far beyond anything that is in the power of the most accomplished artist to transfer to his canvas"* (quoted in Mike King, *Quakernomics: An Ethical Capitalism* [London: Anthem, 2014], 105). That same year, the London *Art-Journal* contemplated the power of Frith's photography: *"In this series we have only the plain unvarnished truth: the actual is absolutely before us, and we know it. There has been here no possibility of either adding or subtracting. The sun is a rare truth-teller"* ([London: James S. Virtue, 1858], 375).

Frith himself seemed to realize this power of his medium: *"There is no effectual substitute for actual travel, but it is my ambition to provide for those to whom circumstances forbid that luxury,* faithful *representations of the scenes I have witnessed, and I shall endeavour to make the simple truthfulness of the Camera, a guide for my Pen"* (quoted in Ali Behdad, *Camera Orientalis: Reflections on Photography of the Middle East* [Chicago: The University of Chicago Press, 2016], 26). In the pages ahead, I hope you'll experience how this has become my desire as well.

Western Wall Plaza and Temple Mount

The Western Wall plaza that we know today hasn't always been pristine.
Here the area is covered in cactus, and dilapidated buildings barely stand.

Well at Ein Rogel

*The crumbling building at the well of Ein Rogel looks up
toward the Old City and the Temple Mount from the south.*

South Wall and Al-Aqsa Mosque

This view looking east from the city walls shows a sparse Mount of Olives and an Old City full of eroded soil, cactus, and overgrowth.

Kidron Valley (Valley of Jehoshaphat)

A portion of the Kidron Valley at the bottom of the Mount of Olives has been used for Jewish burial since biblical times. The traditional monument to David's son Absalom can be seen on the far left. The traditional tomb of King Jehoshaphat is located behind it, though scholars now connect both sites and date them to the first century. On the far right is the traditional tomb of Zechariah, the priest stoned to death by King Joash (2 Chronicles 24:17-22). The middle structure, the tomb of a priestly family, dates to the Hasmonean period.

Temple Mount from the Garden of Gethsemane

*The rugged landscape and Old City from the view
of the Garden's sparsely planted olive trees.*

Eastern Gate from the Temple Mount

*The inside view of the Eastern Gate from the
Temple Mount complex, partially buried in dirt and cactus.*

FRANK MASON GOOD, 1857–70s

Englishman Frank Mason Good got his start in the Middle East in 1857 as an assistant to Francis Frith. After four tours of the area spanning the 1860s and 70s, the first of which was sponsored by Frith, his series of Middle East photos started gaining wide recognition. In 1864 he became a member of the Photographic Society of London. Good's work has been described as *"distinctive and of high technical and artistic merit, especially when the difficulties of working . . . in remote areas is taken into consideration"* (*Encyclopedia of Nineteenth-Century Photography*, ed. John Hannavy [New York: Routledge, 2008], 599).

Al-Aqsa Mosque from the Temple Mount

At the southern end of the Temple Mount stands the Al-Aqsa Mosque.
In the late 1800s, most of the complex was run-down and overgrown.

Mount of Olives

The Mount of Olives with scattered olive groves and no buildings or churches. Notice the small walled area marking the Garden of Gethsemane.

PETER BERGHEIM, 1860s–70s

Bergheim was the first-known resident Jewish photographer in the region, which could perhaps explain the reason for his love of landscape photography. In the 1860s, he opened what is believed to be the first photography studio in the Christian Quarter of the Old City. He also operated a studio in Beirut with fellow photographer Tancrède Dumas. In addition to these endeavors, Bergheim established one of the first modern farms in the Holy Land, as well as its first steam-powered flour mill, located near the Damascus Gate.

Al-Aqsa Mosque and Southwestern Side of Temple Mount

This photo from just inside the Dung Gate on the southeast side of the Old City shows a forgotten city covered in soil and cactus, with a barren Mount of Olives and Mount Scopus in the distance.

Jaffa Gate

AMERICAN COLONY COLLECTION (ACC), 1880s–1940s

More than half the photos in this book are from the American Colony's Eric Matson Collection, and for good reason. It remains to this day one of the most broad, well-documented, and digitized photo collections available of Jerusalem and the region. It has done the world a great service. However, its photos are not the earliest. While the American Colony Collection includes angles similar to the ones we re-created, we used the oldest available photos from the previously featured photographers whenever available. Many of these images predate their counterparts in the American Colony Collection by thirty to seventy years.

Lions' Gate

THE MODERN LENS

The Photos

Possessing an internal compass that points toward adventure and a love for history, my favorite part of this creative process has undoubtedly been the photo shoots. The searching, the struggle, and the ecstasy of finding the exact locations where old-time photographers wrestled their cumbersome gear, driven by a passion to endure the heat and capture this city for the world to see . . . I loved that.

Our shoot was only a week long, but it was busy and physically strenuous. We walked up and down mountains; scaled walls, towers, and endless steps; risked rickety balconies; and traversed hidden side streets all over the city. The team averaged climbing more than 120 floors and walking more than fourteen kilometers, or nine miles, each day.

Yet all physical exhaustion would fade away with the emotional rush of standing on the exact rock outcroppings that Girault de Prangey or Frith stood on some 160 years prior as they gazed at this city. They couldn't have dreamed of what we were looking at from the same vantage points they chose. As a result of their work, we could do ours. As Psalm 48:13-14 instructs, *"Walk around Zion, circle it; count its towers, take note of its ramparts; go through its citadels, that you may recount it to a future age"* (*Jewish Study Bible* [New York: Oxford University Press, 2004], 1336).

Whenever possible, we used the oldest angle of a particular view, even if the original photo was not the most well preserved or the new shot wouldn't reflect the prettiest view of life today. The result is an excellent representation of how photo technology has advanced, as well as how desolate the city truly was, especially prior to the visits of famed travel writers like Mark Twain. It bears repeating: No other people group in human history has any ancient writings that foretell the destruction and future revival of its capital city—not the Romans, the Greeks, the Persians, or the Chinese. Only the Jewish people. Almost 2,600 years after Zechariah's prophecy and after more than a thousand years of desolation, it is undeniable that something is happening in the city of Jerusalem. It's time for you to see for yourself.

Doug and Edden hunting for angles on top of the Jaffa Gate

Finding one of "the *spots*"
in the Old City

PERSONAL ENCOUNTERS

The History and Revival of Jerusalem— in One Moment

Amid the bustling Old City lunchtime crowds, I was enjoying my favorite falafel, casually glancing to my right while taking a bite. Immediately my heart skipped a beat, and I scrambled for my phone to capture the scene unfolding before me. The encounter lasted only a few seconds, but I've been captivated by it ever since.

Being a free-spirited romantic, I don't think I've ever stared at a photo longer. It's an absolute favorite. There is so much to look at: The soldier's surprise two-handed gift as he respectfully leans toward the young woman. His gentle yet direct eye contact, giving her his full attention. Her eyes confidently meeting his while maintaining her guarded body language. Her hesitation beginning to be overtaken, evidenced by her inviting and heartfelt smile while still standing her ground. They look meant for each other.

What's the story behind their encounter? Perhaps he's about to leave with his unit. She's running errands in the city. He had this last-minute surprise planned, and she willingly walked into it. They both know that life in Jerusalem is hard, yet life-giving love is worth just one more moment together, no matter how short. There's the quiet wondering tension in his mind, *Will she miss me while I'm away?* She plans to treasure the roses and even dry them, thinking of him daily, hoping for his soon return.

In reality, your guess is as good as mine. Yet just a short generation ago, a foreign army occupied the Jewish Quarter, desecrating the synagogues and destroying the small plaza where I snapped this picture. Today, in the same spot, the stone pavement is new, and the stucco archways are smooth. Established Jewish families and families that are just beginning are thriving again in safety for the first time in thousands of years.

Have a longer look, and I'll tell you why I love this quick cell phone shot: You can see the history and the restoration of Jerusalem, all in one moment.

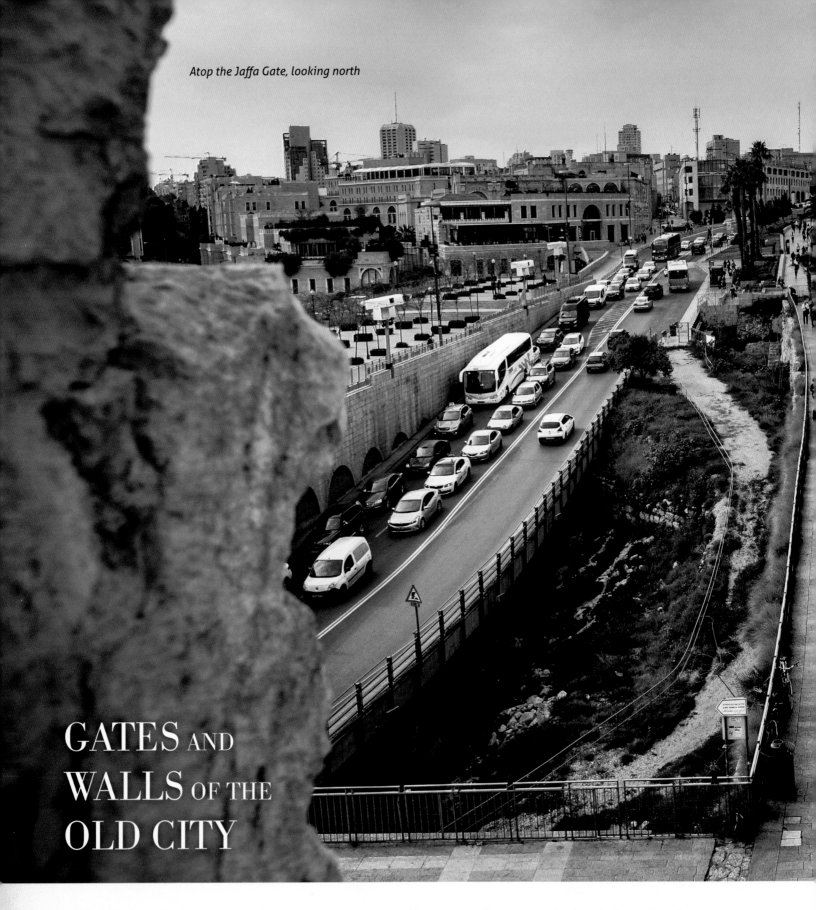

Atop the Jaffa Gate, looking north

GATES AND WALLS OF THE OLD CITY

On at least five different occasions in Jerusalem's history, its walls were added to or completely rebuilt, with each instance changing the dimensions of the city. The walls we see today were built in the sixteenth century by the Ottoman ruler Süleyman the Magnificent. They stand an average of 12 meters (40 feet) in height and extend about 4.5 kilometers (2.8 miles) in length.

> "No one passed in or out [of the gates of Jerusalem]. . . .
> We saw, indeed, no living object, heard no living sound; we found the same void, the same silence . . .
> as we should have expected before the entombed gates of Pompeii or Herculaneum. . . .
> Complete eternal silence reigns in the town, on the highways, in the country."
>
> **Alphonse de Lamartine, nineteenth-century writer and politician,**
> *A Pilgrimage to the Holy Land*, vol. 1 (New York: D. Appleton, 1848), 268, 308

*Jaffa Gate, Demolition to Clear
Area around City Wall,
July 1944
(ACC—Old City, Jaffa Gate)*

Jaffa Gate

The Jaffa Gate gets its name from the port of Jaffa on the coast, which it faces. The road from
Jaffa to this gate was the main thoroughfare into Jerusalem in ancient times. If the Old City
had a front door, the Jaffa Gate would be it. Starting in 1944 and over the course of the next
several decades, old buildings were removed from around the Jaffa Gate, making way for a new
plaza that reveals the grandeur of the Old City's walls.

"Be glad and rejoice forever in what I create; for behold, I create Jerusalem for rejoicing and her people for gladness. I will also rejoice in Jerusalem and be glad in My people; and there will no longer be heard in her the voice of weeping and the sound of crying."

Isaiah 65:18-19, NASB

Jaffa Gate,
1860
(Bergheim)

Jaffa Gate,
1907
(ACC—Old City, Jaffa Gate)

Jerusalem: the city which miraculously transforms man into pilgrim; no one can enter it and go away unchanged."

Elie Wiesel, renowned writer,
Nobel Prize recipient and Holocaust survivor,
A Beggar in Jerusalem

Tower of David (Citadel),
1844
(Girault de Prangey)

“ *See, I have engraved you on the palms of my hands;*

your walls are ever before me."

Isaiah 49:16

Tower of David (Citadel)

Guarding the upper portion of the Old City for centuries, the Tower of David is one of the most recognizable landmarks in Jerusalem. In 1917, British General Edmund Allenby walked victoriously through the Jaffa Gate and stood on the steps of the Tower of David to officially proclaim an end to four hundred years of Ottoman rule in Jerusalem. Today it is home to the beautiful Tower of David Museum and serves as a prime venue for special events.

Zion Gate,
1898–1914
(ACC—Old City, Gates and Walls)

Zion Gate

In the pre-1948 photo, the stonework appears nearly pristine compared to the gate's present battered condition. During Israel's War of Independence, the Jordanian Arab Legion, supported by Arab irregulars, began attacking the Jewish Quarter inside the gate. Jewish forces tried desperately to defend the 1,500 residents, but on May 28, 1948, the Quarter finally had to be surrendered, with most of the Jews inside granted safe passage to the Israeli sector of Jerusalem. Today the facade shown here, heavily pockmarked by bullet and shell holes, bears the scars of that fighting.

> *In the din and tumult of the age . . . the still small voice of Jerusalem remains our only music.*"

Israel Zangwill, British author, cultural Zionist, and political activist,
The Voice of Jerusalem (New York: Macmillan, 1921), 8–9

Al-Aqsa Mosque and Mount of Olives,
1898–1914
(ACC—Al-Aqsa Mosque)

South Wall

For centuries until the 1900s, much of the area near the

Old City had been "plowed like a field," as the prophet foretold.

As you can see, today the restoration has begun.

Zion will be plowed like a field, Jerusalem will become a heap of rubble, the temple hill a mound overgrown with thickets."

Micah 3:12

*South Wall and Al-Aqsa Mosque,
1857
(Frith)*

" *Foreigners will rebuild your walls, and their
kings will serve you. Though in anger I struck
you, in favor I will show you compassion."*

Isaiah 60:10

" *I propose to Your Majesties that all the profit to be derived from my enterprise should be used for the recovery of Jerusalem.*"

Christopher Columbus, Italian explorer and navigator,
quoted in Joshua Prawer, *The World of the Crusaders* (New York: Quadrangle, 1973), 152

Doug and Edden on the Ramparts Walk of Jerusalem's Old City walls, looking for the next perfect angle

PERSONAL ENCOUNTERS
Edden's 11:11

Most tattoos have a fascinating story behind them. What makes something so important to a person that they would permanently ink a reminder of it onto their body? While on a break one afternoon with *Jerusalem Rising*'s photographer, Edden Ram, I fully expected to swing open the door of interesting conversation when I asked him about his unique tattoo.

"So, Edden, tell me about your 11:11 tattoo on the back of your right arm," I casually said while we were seated at a Jerusalem coffee shop.

Edden started to smile as one who was recalling a life event and didn't know how to keep their answer brief. *"It's a number I started seeing as a kid. It has become sort of a spiritual compass for me."*

"That's interesting," I replied, my mind already turning. *"Did you start seeing that number before or after you moved to Israel?"*

"Before we moved here . . . Why?" he said with a perplexed look, not expecting that question.

"As you know," I replied, *"I teach around the world on Bible prophecy coming to pass in our lifetimes through the nation of Israel. One of those topics has to do with 11:11 . . . Isaiah 11:11. It says that God will recover his people 'a second time' with his hand. The amazing thing is that when Isaiah spoke this, the Jewish people had not yet been scattered from the Land the first time, and God was already talking about restoring them back to the Land 'a second time.' The first time he brought them back here was after the Babylonian exile, when Ezra and Nehemiah led them. They were scattered a second time after the Roman conquest almost two thousand years ago, and the second time they are being regathered to the Land is . . . right now."*

With a recently discovered Jewish background as part of my own family's history, I paused for a moment so it could sink in for both of us.

"That's why I wondered when you started seeing '11:11.' Perhaps it was God stirring your heart at a young age to bring you back to where you belong. That is the message of this photo book—that God is reviving Jerusalem to bring us back to where we belong. And here we are having this conversation outside a busy Jerusalem coffee shop as kids run by. You've seen the old pictures—this city has been a desolate dump for centuries, up until about fifty years ago. And yet here we are, back from the nations a second time, sharing a coffee."

I have been lecturing on this topic for years, but in that moment, it felt like an unexpected heart revelation for both of us. We remained quiet for a moment with raised eyebrows, a sense of awe, and a renewed focus to accurately re-create these old photos as best as we possibly could for this book. Every now and then, I have a sense of being in the right place at the right time, doing the right thing. This was one of those moments, and all because of a tattoo.

ISAIAH 11:11

"It shall come to pass in that day, that the Lord shall set his hand again the second time to recover the remnant of his people." (KJV)

Dung Gate (Interior),
1940–46
(ACC—Old City, Gates and Walls)

Dung Gate

"Dung Gate," as it's translated according to the traditional Jewish name, refers to a gate in the south wall of the city that is mentioned in Nehemiah 2:13. It's thought that garbage from ancient Jerusalem, including ashes from Temple sacrifices, was brought out of the city through this gate. After the Jordanians sealed the west-facing Jaffa Gate, they redesigned and widened the Dung Gate in 1953 to allow motor vehicles access into the Old City, especially to their military post at the Tower of David (Citadel).

Dung Gate (Exterior)

> *By night [Nehemiah] went out through the Valley Gate toward the Jackal Well and the Dung Gate, examining the walls of Jerusalem, which had been broken down, and its gates, which had been destroyed by fire."*

Nehemiah 2:13

Eastern Gate,
approximately 1890s
(ACC—The Early Footsteps)

Eastern Gate

When Süleyman the Magnificent rebuilt the city walls, he ordered the sealing of the Eastern Gate (also known as the Golden Gate) and the planting of a Muslim graveyard in front of it. It was believed he did this as an affront to the Jews since the Scriptures foretell their Messiah will enter Jerusalem from the Mount of Olives, to the east. A sealed gate would prevent Messiah's physical entrance, and passing through a graveyard would make him unclean by Torah standards. Ironically, by doing so Süleyman fulfilled the prophecy in Ezekiel 44:1-3, foretelling a time when this gate would be shut.

Open up, ancient gates! Open up, ancient doors, and let the King of glory enter. Who is the King of glory? The LORD of Heaven's Armies—he is the King of glory."

Psalm 24:9-10, NLT

Lions' Gate, 1844
(Girault de Prangey)

Lions' Gate

Of all the times Jerusalem has been conquered, only twice has it not fallen from the north. Ironically, each instance was from the east and by Jewish hands. The first was when David's general Joab entered through the water tunnel three thousand years ago, seizing the city from the Jebusites. The second was in 1967, when the Israel Defense Forces took the Old City from the Jordanians, entering through the Lions' Gate. As previously mentioned, Bible prophecy states that the Messiah will also enter Jerusalem from the east, after his arrival on the Mount of Olives.

On that day [the LORD's] feet will stand on the Mount of Olives, east of Jerusalem, and the Mount of Olives will be split in two from east to west."

Zechariah 14:4

North Wall,
1898–1914
(ACC—Old City, Gates and Walls)

North Wall

❝*May it please you to prosper Zion, to build up the walls of Jerusalem.*"

Psalm 51:18

> *How long will there be weeping in Zion and lamentation in Jerusalem? Have mercy on Zion and build anew the walls of Jerusalem!"*

"Dirge for the Ninth of Av,"
T. Carmi, ed., *The Penguin Book of Hebrew Verse,*
(New York: Penguin Books, 1981), 204

*Herod's Gate,
1940–46
(ACC—Old City, Gates and Walls)*

Herod's Gate

Herod's Gate is the northern entrance of today's Muslim Quarter of the Old City. The gate is named after the traditional location of a palace of Herod Antipas that once stood nearby.

Pray for the peace of Jerusalem: 'May those who love you be secure. May there be peace within your walls and security within your citadels.'"

Psalm 122:6-7

Damascus Gate

The Damascus Gate, built by the Ottomans in 1538, is one of the most ornate, decorative gates of the Old City. As the Jaffa Gate faces the port of Jaffa, the Damascus Gate on the north side of the Old City faces Damascus. It's one of the first gates travelers would have seen coming from the north, whether in ancient times or up until the Ottoman Empire. Under this "modern" construction are remains of a massive fortified gate from Roman times, which suggests its prominence through the centuries.

"Pass through, pass through the gates! Prepare the way for the people. Build up, build up the highway! Remove the stones. Raise a banner for the nations."

Isaiah 62:10

New Gate

The New Gate, aptly named, was added in 1887 and is the most recent addition to the Old City's walls and gates. The New Gate provided access to new buildings on the north side of the Old City.

" The LORD loves the gates of Zion more than all the other dwellings of Jacob. Glorious things are said of you, city of God."

Psalm 87:2-3

*Ramparts Walk, View of Old City from Wall,
1910–20
(ACC—Old City, Gates and Walls)*

I have posted watchmen on your walls, Jerusalem; they will never be silent day or night. You who call on the Lᴏʀᴅ, give yourselves no rest, and give him no rest till he establishes Jerusalem and makes her the praise of the earth."

Isaiah 62:6-7

Following the light in the Old City

OLD CITY

> ❝*The nations will walk by its light, and the kings of the earth will bring their splendor into it. On no day will its gates ever be shut, for there will be no night there.*❞
>
> Revelation 21:24-25

"The Jewish connection to Jerusalem is an ancient and powerful one. Judaism made Jerusalem a holy city over three thousand years ago, and through all that time Jews remained steadfast to it."

Daniel Pipes, Middle East historian and writer,
Nothing Abides: Perspectives on the Middle East and Islam
(London: Routledge, 2017), 11

City of David

Discoveries at the City of David excavations have continued to stun archaeologists and visitors alike.

While this steeply stepped structure was once considered a portion of an ancient wall, further excavations

suggest it served as a retaining wall for a large stone building many researchers believe was King David's palace.

"For the State of Israel there has always been and always will be one capital only—Jerusalem the Eternal. Thus it was 3,000 years ago— and thus it will be, we believe, until the end of time."

David Ben-Gurion, speech to the Knesset,

December 13, 1949,

"Prime Minister Ben-Gurion on Jerusalem," jewishvirtuallibrary.org

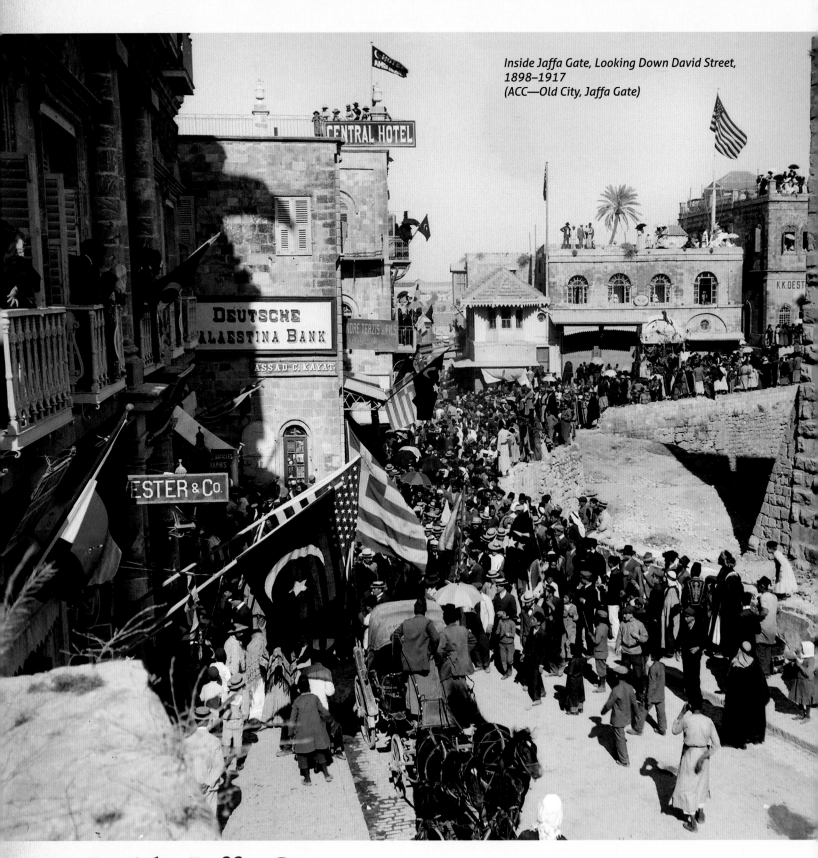

Inside Jaffa Gate, Looking Down David Street, 1898–1917
(ACC—Old City, Jaffa Gate)

Inside Jaffa Gate

"I rejoiced with those who said to me, 'Let us go to the house of the LORD.' Our feet are standing in your gates, Jerusalem."

Psalm 122:1-2

*Jaffa Gate from Inside the Old City,
1908–14
(ACC—Old City, Jaffa Gate)*

In the early 1900s, the Ottomans built the Jaffa Gate clock tower in honor of the sultan's twenty-fifth year of rule. The tower remained until 1922, when the Ottomans conceded governance to the British, who had conquered the city in 1917.

"Jerusalem is a port city on the shore of eternity."

Yehuda Amichai, 1924–2000, Israeli poet,

The Selected Poetry of Yehuda Amichai,

(Berkeley, CA: University of California Press, 2013), 54

Pool of Hezekiah

Once a small quarry for the construction of an ancient nearby defensive wall, this site was later converted for water usage during the time of King Hezekiah. The reservoir held water until recent times.

*Jerusalem is built like a city that is
closely compacted together."*

Psalm 122:3

> The king of Assyria sent his supreme commander, his chief officer and his field commander with a large army, from Lachish to King Hezekiah at Jerusalem. They came up to Jerusalem and stopped at the aqueduct of the Upper Pool, on the road to the Washerman's Field."
>
> 1 Kings 18:17

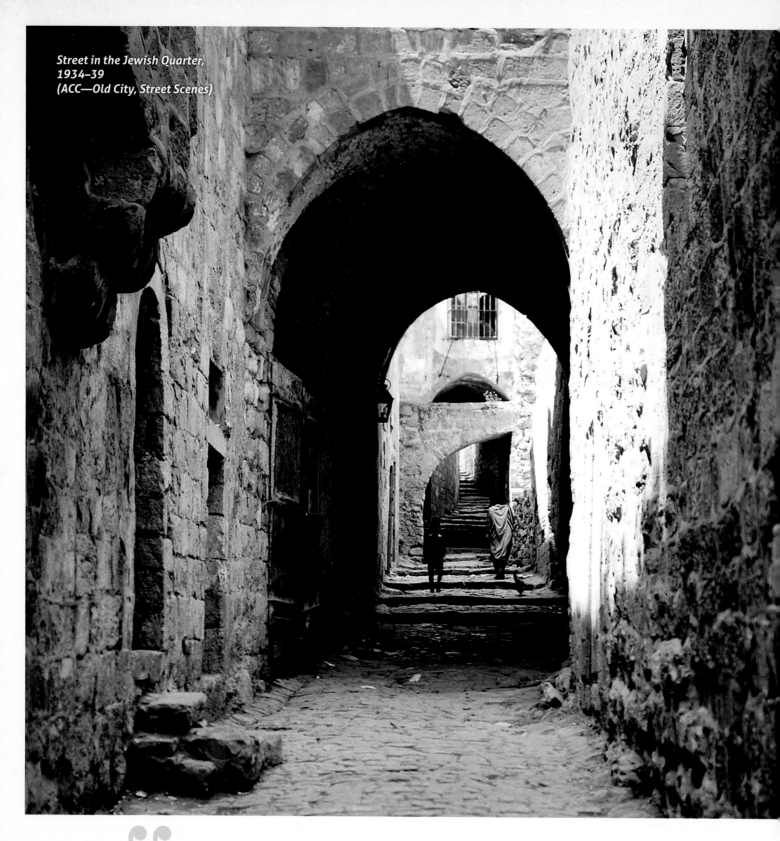

Street in the Jewish Quarter, 1934–39 (ACC—Old City, Street Scenes)

❝ *The streets are roughly and badly paved with stone, and are tolerably crooked—enough so to make each street appear to close together constantly and come to an end about a hundred yards ahead of a pilgrim as long as he chooses to walk in it. . . . Since a cat can jump across them without the least inconvenience, it is hardly necessary to state that such streets are too narrow for carriages. These vehicles can not navigate the Holy City.* ❞

Mark Twain, 1867,
The Innocents Abroad, 558–59

Jewish Quarter

Today, visitors, residents, and local children are pouring through this maze of streets in ways Mark Twain could have never imagined.

" *In the towns of Judah and the streets of Jerusalem that are deserted . . . there will be heard once more the sounds of joy and gladness.*"

Jeremiah 33:10-11

PERSONAL ENCOUNTERS
Ari the Guide

Our collection included some stunning pictures of early excavations in one of the oldest parts of Jerusalem—the original City of David, where King David built his palace—so I contacted the directors there to help me identify the exact spots the photos were taken from. While I know Jerusalem pretty well, there are still some locations that I have no idea how to find. In turn, the directors connected me with "the best historical guide in Jerusalem."

"Ari knows everything; he is de best," I was confidently told in a thick accent that left me wondering if I was talking to a salesman in an Old City souvenir shop. Yet given that I had set aside only one week to reshoot all the old photos we'd chosen, we needed the help of an expert.

Hopeful yet mildly skeptical, I needed to test such high praise. After sending Ari a brief email introducing myself and my goals, I forwarded to him six black-and-white photos from the Old City of Jerusalem, taken

Ari, revealing to our team what was hidden in plain sight

between 1844 and the early 1900s, and asked for help locating their sites. Within ten minutes, he responded.

"This one is taken from the valley floor near the old spring . . ."

"This archway is still there, but it's hard to see with all the other buildings and electric cables . . ."

"This building was torn down in the mid-1900s and no longer exists . . ."

Suddenly he had my full attention. I scheduled him for a Sunday afternoon, his only available four-hour window during the week.

Ari showed up on time, wearing his guide badge, a quirky smile, and a kippah under his bucket-style sun hat. He also brought a headful of information that rivaled *Encyclopaedia Britannica*. He would take a quick look at an aged photo on our iPad, then say, *"Okay, that's over here"*—and off we went, almost drowning in

his historical lectures. The pace of his walk equaled my daughter's jog, his stamina on the steep paths around Jerusalem rivaled a mountain goat's (on steroids), and his historical knowledge of the landscape and archaeology was second to none.

Ari was our "divine appointment" for accomplishing our mission in the time frame we had. We went down to the Kidron Valley floor and back up to the Old City through a "shortcut" of biblical graves. He led us through back alleys, side streets, and corridors I didn't know existed in the Old City. In a maze of ancient streets that, at first glance, all look the same, we found the exact archways featured in 120-year-old pictures.

According to our fitness-tracker app, we walked 14.7 kilometers (9.1 miles), took more than 20,500 steps, and climbed 126 floors that day while re-creating some amazing shots. I had to admit, the guys at the City of David weren't wrong—Ari did know everything.

Via Dolorosa

The Via Dolorosa is the traditional route that Jesus took on the way to his crucifixion. Its winding path is marked by fourteen "stations" where pilgrims pray and remember a specific event that happened along his journey.

*The soldiers led Jesus away into the palace
(that is, the Praetorium) and called together
the whole company of soldiers."*

Mark 15:16

Via Dolorosa,
Fourth Station of the Cross,
1898–1934
(ACC—Via Dolorosa)

At the fourth station of the cross, pilgrims stop to reflect on the tradition that Jesus met his mother here on the way to the crucifixion site. While this meeting is not recorded in the New Testament, a sixth-century mosaic marks the location as a place of remembrance.

> " As a mother comforts her child, so will I comfort you; and you will be comforted over Jerusalem."
>
> Isaiah 66:13

Via Dolorosa,
Fifth Station of the Cross,
1898–1914
(ACC—Via Dolorosa)

The fifth station of the cross remembers the traditional spot where Jesus fell under the weight of the cross and Simon of Cyrene was conscripted from the crowd to carry it for him: "As they were coming out, they found a man of Cyrene named Simon, whom they pressed into service to bear His cross" (Matthew 27:32, NASB).

The houses are generally two stories high, built strongly of masonry, whitewashed or plastered outside, and have a cage of wooden lattice-work projecting in front of every window. To reproduce a Jerusalem street, it would only be necessary to up-end a chicken-coop and hang it before each window in an alley of American houses."

Mark Twain, 1867,
The Innocents Abroad, 558

Via Dolorosa,
Sixth Station of the Cross,
1898–1914
(ACC—Via Dolorosa)

Though the sixth station of the cross is also not recorded in the New Testament, pilgrims believe that here a woman named Veronica wiped Jesus' face with a handkerchief, which then miraculously transformed to hold his image. Some allege the handkerchief has been preserved at the Vatican since AD 707.

<blockquote>
Burst into songs of joy together, you ruins of Jerusalem, for the Lord has comforted his people, he has redeemed Jerusalem."
</blockquote>

Isaiah 52:9

Church of the Holy Sepulchre

This famed church is built around the traditional site of the crucifixion and tomb of Jesus. Traditions from early church history state that Christians were gathering here to pray by the middle of the first century. While the church's original foundations date to the early Byzantine period in the third century, it has been rebuilt and expanded several times since then.

Church of the Holy Sepulchre,
1950s
(ACC—Church of the Holy Sepulchre)

The View East from the Tower of David, 1910–20
(ACC—Views of the City)

> *The view from the top of David's Tower is extensive, embracing the whole town, the Mount of Olives, the Dead Sea, and the Mountains of Moab—a pleasant sight to feast the eyes upon for half an hour before the sun goes down."*

Sir Charles William Wilson, 1864, English explorer and researcher,
Picturesque Palestine, Sinai, and Egypt (New York: D. Appleton, 1881), 11

View from the Tower of David

The Tower of David, found at the Jaffa Gate on the western side of the Old City, provides a beautifully unique vantage point of the width of the city as you look east toward the Temple Mount and Mount of Olives. In the distance, the lone Tower of the Ascension marks the site traditionally believed to be the place where Jesus ascended into heaven.

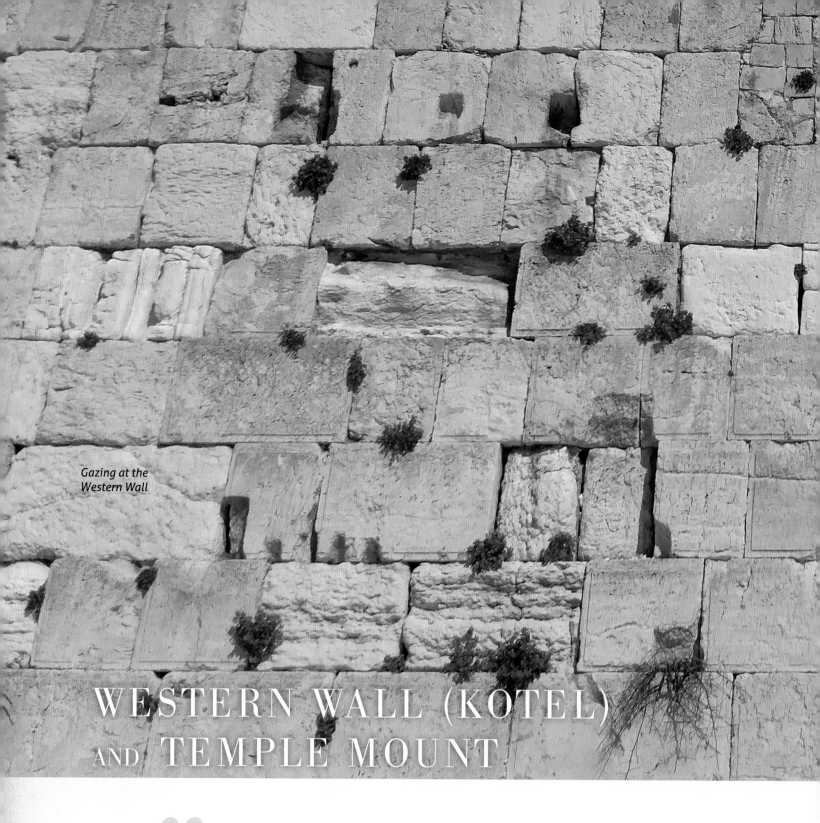

Gazing at the Western Wall

WESTERN WALL (KOTEL) AND TEMPLE MOUNT

" *No sight in Jerusalem affected me more than [the Western Wall].* "

Edward Wilmot Blyden, African American author,

From West Africa to Palestine (Freetown, Sierra Leone: T. J. Sawyer, 1873), 181

Now my eyes will be open and my ears attentive to the prayers offered in this place. I have chosen and consecrated this temple so that my Name may be there forever. My eyes and my heart will always be there."

2 Chronicles 7:15-16

Western Wall (Kotel), 1910–20 (ACC—Western Wall)

PERSONAL ENCOUNTERS

Gentile Groom at the Western Wall

I have been to the Western Wall dozens of times. For me, it never gets old. I'm always struck by the biblical promises connected to this location, its modern history, the people who come, and their sense of respect for the divine. It's all part of Jerusalem's unfolding story.

When I have the opportunity, I often stand at the wall for my own time of meditation and prayer, then pull up one of the plastic chairs to watch the devotion of the regulars and the wonder-filled emotions of first-timers as they step into such a treasured place.

On one particular day, I chose a shaded spot in the middle of the men's section that was close enough to still be in the mix of the coming-and-going crowds—but not too close to distract those praying at the Wall. Soon I noticed an older American man about three or

four meters (ten feet) to my left. He was wearing a baseball hat, sunglasses, and an amazed countenance and had chosen a similar approach as I had, finding a seat to soak everything in. After overhearing a few people interact with him and seeing the look on his face turn to confusion, I struck up a friendly conversation, asking if he was okay.

Gary, a Gentile, had an interesting story. Deeply in love, he was newly engaged to a beautiful Israeli woman he'd met in Brooklyn, New York, and was now on his first trip to Israel to meet her family and learn about her Jewish heritage. We casually talked about how they met, if they had a wedding date set, and whether they were considering living in Israel after they were married. He never anticipated he would meet and fall in love with an Israeli woman, nor had he ever experienced a desire to come to Israel. Yet now that he was sitting in awe in the shadow of the Western Wall, his perspective was changing.

"I . . . I never expected . . . that I would feel this way in this place," he stammered, slowly struggling for words. *"Who knows, maybe we could live here. . . . But at the very least, I already would like to return."*

I smiled, knowing full well that this city has an indescribable effect on people. After some more chatting, I realized I was simply a distraction to his ongoing experience. I gave him my heartfelt congratulations, but since there was nothing else to say, I left him to ponder his unanticipated holy moment. I had no doubt that, just like many others from the nations, he would be back.

Western Wall (Kotel),
View from the South,
1940–46
(ACC—Western Wall)

> The people in prayer thrust their hands into the interstices [between the stones],
> and also push as far into the crevices as they can, prayers they have written to God.
> . . . It is a most remarkable sight; these people all thronging the pavement, and
> wailing so intensely, that often the tears roll down their faces."

Charles Warren, 1867, English archaeologist,
Underground Jerusalem, 367–68

"Once you have lived a moment at the Wall, you never go away."

Abraham Joshua Heschel, twentieth-century Jewish theologian,

Israel: An Echo of Eternity (New York: Farrar, Straus, and Giroux, 1969), 21

Southwest Side of the Temple Mount Area,
1860
(Frith—Google Arts and Culture, J. Paul Getty Museum)

Western Wall Plaza Entrance

Left in disarray and forgotten for centuries, the area known today as the entryway
to the Western Wall plaza was once overtaken by a sea of dirt and cactus.

"*I left my family, I forsook my house. . . . With them, my heart and my eyes will dwell forever. . . . But the loss of all else which delighted my eyes is compensated by my present joy in a day passed within thy courts, Oh Jerusalem! visiting the ruins of the Temple and crying over the ruined Sanctuary, where it is granted me to caress thy stones, to fondle thy dust, and to weep over thy ruins. I wept bitterly, but I found joy in my heart. I rent my garments, but I found solace in doing so.*"

Nachmanides (Moshe ben Nachman), thirteenth-century Spanish rabbi and Talmudic scholar,
quoted in Franz Kobler, ed., *Letters of Jews through the Ages*, vol. 1
(New York: East and West Library/The Jewish Publication Society, 1978), 227

Al-Aqsa Mosque and Mount of Olives,
1898–1914
(ACC)

Southern End

This view of the southern end of the Temple Mount complex, captured from where the Davidson Center would one day stand, shows the area covered with wild cactus. In the background is a desolate Mount of Olives, the famed location for viewing Jerusalem and of multiple events in the Scriptures.

" *It is I who says of Jerusalem, 'She shall be inhabited!' And of the cities of Judah, ' They shall be built.' And I will raise up her ruins again."*

Isaiah 44:26, NASB

Area South of the Temple Mount,
June 1933
(Israel Antiquities Authority, Photographer Unknown)

Less than one hundred years ago, the area just south of the Temple Mount was used as a vegetable patch, as seen above. Today this same area, now called the Davidson Center (or Jerusalem Archaeological Park), has been excavated. Some profound biblical treasures were revealed, including more than fifty mikvahs near the southern Temple steps (for ritual cleansing—the Christian concept of baptism comes from this practice) and an ancient clay seal with the name of Hezekiah, king of Judah, inscribed on it.

In the third year of Hoshea son of Elah king of Israel, Hezekiah son of Ahaz king of Judah began to reign. He was twenty-five years old when he became king, and he reigned in Jerusalem twenty-nine years."

2 Kings 18:1-2

The Triple Gate,
1910–20
(ACC—Temple Mount)

" *Cauliflowers… grow to an enormous size and in great profusion*
on the slopes of Ophel, the finest I have ever seen."

Charles Warren, 1867, English archaeologist,
Underground Jerusalem (London: Richard Bentley and Son, 1876), 89

Huldah Gates

Pictured above are the rebuilt eastern set of gates for the structure collectively known in other rabbinical writings as the Huldah Gates, though the meaning of the name is unclear. The original gates served as entrances to the Temple complex in the first and second centuries BC (Hasmonean era) and were reconstructed by Herod during the late Second Temple period. Walled up since the Middle Ages, the gates are on the southern side of the Temple Mount in the location referred to in the Bible as the Ophel—the area extending upward from the City of David.

Temple Mount and Dome of the Rock,
1844
(Girault de Prangey)

❝ *Even though the Sanctuary is today in ruins . . . we are obliged*
to reverence it in the same manner as when it was standing. . . .
For even though it is in ruins, its sanctity endures.❞

Maimonides, twelfth-century Jewish philosopher and Torah scholar,
The Book of Temple Service 28–30, trans. Mendell Lewittes,
quoted in *The Holy Land* (Oxford: Oxford University Press, 2008), 89

Son of man, this is the place of my throne and the place for the soles of my feet. This is where I will live among the Israelites forever."

Ezekiel 43:7

*Temple Mount,
1844
(Girault de Prangey)*

PERSONAL ENCOUNTERS
This Is My Home

A trusted Palestinian friend, Ahmed, lives in East Jerusalem and drives a taxi. When Jewish tour guides tell me I will not be able to get somewhere due to "political reasons," I call Ahmed. He knows people everywhere, as well he should. His family has lived in the same Jerusalem village for almost two centuries, dating back to when just a few families made up his small town. In the Arab culture, respect, honor, and a good name are everything. As a leader in his community, he possesses them all.

For example, at one location during this shoot, a Jewish guide told me in a concerned tone that the angle for the photo above was from inside what is now an Arab school. He confided that he was inside only once, ten years ago, and that I might need to give up re-creating that angle due to the current political climate. I quietly said *"Okay,"* nodded, and smiled.

Then I called Ahmed. After telling him what I wanted to do, and where, he immediately responded, *"No problem. When do you want to go?"*—as casually as if we were planning to meet at the corner coffee shop. Within twelve hours, Ahmed was greeting us with hearty smiles and traditional Arab cheek kisses. Soon we were standing inside this school at almost the exact spot French photographer Joseph-Philibert Girault de Prangey stood 175 years before, capturing an angle of the Temple Mount few have ever seen.

In this part of the world, relationship is everything.

This rarely seen angle of the Temple Mount was taken from inside an Arab school that our friend Ahmed gave us access to.

Later, while enjoying a thick Turkish coffee at Ahmed's house, we began talking about life in Jerusalem.

"People are people," he said in thickly Arabic-accented English. *"Everyone wants to live in peace, but there are some who make that difficult."*

After a thoughtful drag on a cigarette and a sip of potent coffee that looked like used motor oil, he continued. *"I've been to the US and to places in Europe, and those places are nice. I have been offered millions and millions of dollars for my home . . . but I want to live here."*

Ahmed's family endured the harsh Ottoman Empire, Westernization attempts under the British Mandate, and nineteen years of destructive Jordanian rule. Then came the growing prosperity of Israeli sovereignty. Despite the current challenges, personal struggles, and disagreements that many Arabs have with Israel's government, Ahmed confided that the last twenty-five years of Palestinian rule has been awful. Most Palestinians quietly recognize that Israeli control remains the best option.

"I love it here," he said. *"This is my home. There is nowhere else I'd rather be. We can all live together."*

" At that time they will call Jerusalem 'The Throne of the LORD,' and all the nations will be gathered to it, to Jerusalem, for the name of the LORD; nor will they walk anymore after the stubbornness of their evil heart. In those days the house of Judah will walk with the house of Israel, and they will come together from the land of the north to the land that I gave your fathers as an inheritance."

Jeremiah 3:17-18, NASB

*Al-Aqsa Mosque
from the Temple Mount,
1857
(Good)*

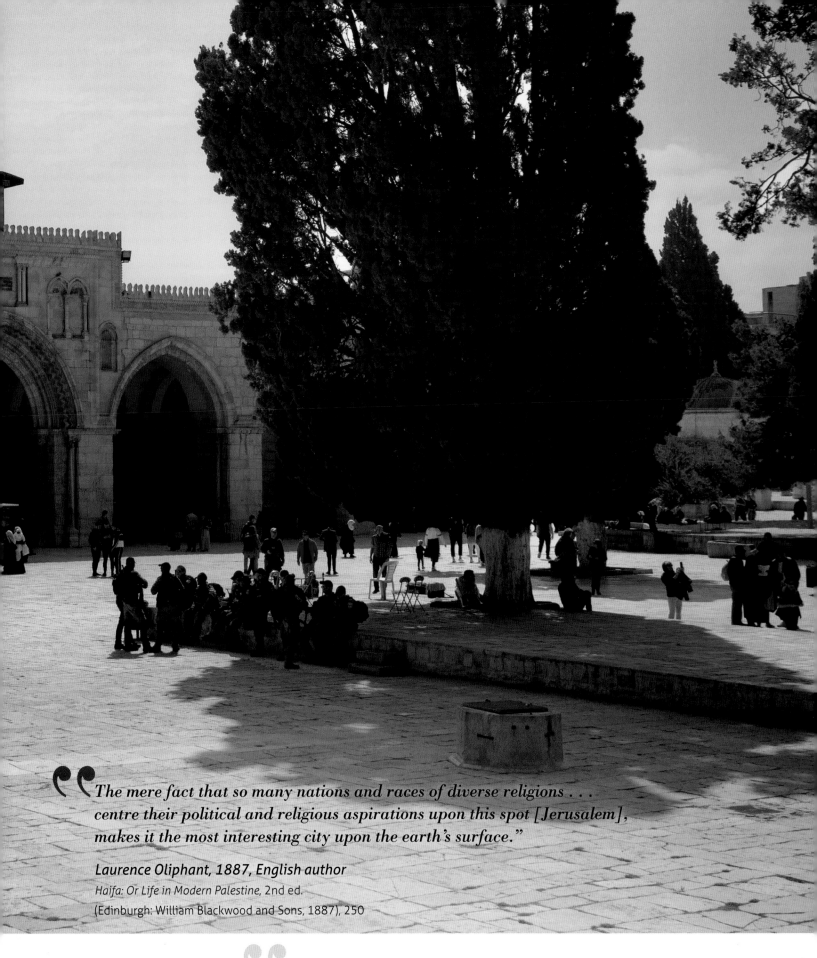

" *The mere fact that so many nations and races of diverse religions . . .*
centre their political and religious aspirations upon this spot [Jerusalem],
makes it the most interesting city upon the earth's surface."

Laurence Oliphant, 1887, English author
Haifa: Or Life in Modern Palestine, 2nd ed.
(Edinburgh: William Blackwood and Sons, 1887), 250

" *A prayer in the Mosque al-Aqsa is worth ten thousand prayers.*"

Ibn al-Firkah al-Fazari, fourteenth-century Muslim scholar,
quoted in Charles D. Matthews, *Palestine—Mohammedan Holy Land*
(New Haven, CT: Yale University Press, 1949), 4

*Eastern Gate from the Temple Mount,
1857
(Good)*

❝ *Jerusalem is the eternal mother of the Jewish People,
precious and beloved even in its desolation."*

Chaim Weizmann, first president of Israel,
quoted in Meron Medzini, ed.,
Israel's Foreign Relations: Selected Documents, vol. 1
(Israel: Ministry for Foreign Affairs, 1976), 220

Eastern Gate

> *The glory of the LORD entered the temple through the gate facing east."*
>
> Ezekiel 43:4

View of Hebrew University on Mount Scopus

NEW CITY

❝ *This is what the L*ORD *Almighty says: 'My towns will again overflow with prosperity, and the L*ORD *will again comfort Zion and choose Jerusalem.'"*

Zechariah 1:17

"In Jerusalem are all manner of learned men and doctors, and for this reason the hearts of men of intelligence yearn towards her."

Mukaddasi, AD 985, Muslim historian, geographer, and native of Jerusalem,
Description of Syria, Including Palestine, trans. Guy Le Strange
(London: Palestine Pilgrims' Text Society, 1886), 35

West of the Old City

Montefiore Windmill, located just to the left of center in these photos, is a symbol of the first Jewish neighborhood outside Jerusalem's walls—Mishkenot Sha'ananim, constructed around 1860. English Jewish philanthropist Sir Moses Montefiore established the neighborhood to alleviate the housing shortage in the Old City and built the windmill a few years earlier to ensure the inhabitants would have a livelihood. Lacking sufficient wind, the mill never operated on a regular basis and broke down frequently. Soon it was made obsolete by steam-powered mills.

Now restored, the windmill stands 15 meters (50 feet) high and serves as a reminder of the new city's beginnings. It is surrounded by vintage homes and stone streets, with office and residential buildings standing in the foreground on the influential King David Street. Just behind this camera angle is the King David Hotel, known as the preferred lodging for visiting foreign dignitaries and world leaders.

View North from the YMCA Tower,
1934–39
(ACC—New City)

Northwest of the Old City

The only matching aspect in these then-and-now photos is the dome of the Ethiopian monastery, part of the Ethiopian Orthodox Church in Jerusalem that was inaugurated in 1893. Today the landscape is filled with luxury hotels and business offices.

> *As a result of the historic catastrophe in which Titus of Rome destroyed Jerusalem and Israel was exiled from its land, I was born in one of the cities of the Exile. But always I regarded myself as one who was born in Jerusalem.*"

S. Y. Agnon, Israeli author,
1966 Nobel Prize acceptance speech,
"Shmuel Agnon Banquet Speech," nobelprize.org

*Mount Zion, Hinnom Valley, and Wilderness
from the YMCA Tower,
1934–39
(ACC—Views of the City)*

> *Indeed, of Zion it will be said, 'This one and that one were born in her,
> and the Most High himself will establish her.' The Lord will write in the
> register of the peoples: 'This one was born in Zion.'"*

Psalm 87:5-6

"Jerusalem is a small town of big things; and the average modern city is a big town full of small things. All the most important and interesting powers in history are here gathered within the area of a quiet village; and if they are not always friends, at least they are necessarily neighbours."

G. K. Chesterton, twentieth-century Catholic writer,
The New Jerusalem (New York: George H. Doran, 1921), 122

*Hinnom Valley from the West,
1910–20
(ACC—Views of the City)*

Hinnom Valley

The Hinnom Valley played a significant part in Israel's biblical history. While it was a
natural southern defense for the city of Jerusalem, perhaps its most unfortunate mention is
as the location where children were sacrificed to the false god Molech (Jeremiah 32:35).
The modern village of Silwan can be seen in the distance.

" *Comfort, comfort my people, says your God. Speak tenderly to Jerusalem, and proclaim to her that her hard service has been completed, that her sin has been paid for, that she has received from the Lord's hand double for all her sins.*"

Isaiah 40:1-2

PERSONAL ENCOUNTERS
Café Confessions

One evening after a long day of photo shoots, Edden and I went to a popular café in Jerusalem to review the day and plan for the next. Sarah, a young blonde server with a clearly American accent, struck up a conversation with us since it was still relatively early by Middle Eastern standards. She began by asking us where we were from—not an unusual question in such an international city. The more we chatted about what had brought us to Israel, Jerusalem, and specifically that café, the

more her own fascinating story began pouring out. As unique as it was, it is one that I hear quite often, minus the specific personal details.

Sarah grew up in Oregon, and as many young Western Jews do, she first came to Israel on a Birthright Israel tour. This organization brings young people from Jewish communities throughout the world to Israel, connecting them with the land of their ancestors and their heritage. Something happened while she was in Israel: Israel began happening in her.

At age twenty-two, after ending a relationship and feeling like she needed a fresh start, Sarah responded to the longing for Israel that had quietly taken root in her heart. Soon she took a step on her own, making *aliyah* (the term used for Jewish people returning to the Land and becoming Israeli citizens) and immersing herself in Israeli culture.

By the time we met her, Sarah had been living in Jerusalem for more than a year and was making her own way. She talked about how she had found the job at the restaurant and made new friends, about how she was struggling with Hebrew language school and had just gotten a puppy. But I was still waiting to hear the real reason for her solo move halfway around the world from her family and hometown, so I simply asked an open-ended question.

"Tell me—why Israel, and why Jerusalem?"

Without skipping a beat, she smiled wryly and shrugged her shoulders, then said the words I hear from so many

others and that few are able to explain.

"Because I belong here. I feel safe here. This feels like home to me more than any other place in the world, and there is no other place that I'd rather be."

At this comment, Edden began chuckling and said with a sense of wonderment, *"What other country on earth do you hear that about? All my friends say the same thing."* I can't deny that I feel the same way about this city and nation.

Just like Sarah, Jewish people throughout the world continue to feel the pull to the Land, and they are responding.

*Rockefeller Museum,
1934–39
(ACC—New City)*

❝ *Jerusalem, get up and shine! Your Light is coming!
The Glory of the L*ORD *will shine on you. . . . All the
riches from across the seas will be set before you.
The riches of the nations will come to you.*"

Isaiah 60:1, 5, ERV

Rockefeller Museum

Named after the famed American businessman and philanthropist John D. Rockefeller Jr., who agreed to help finance the museum with a gift of $2 million ($38 million today), this historic landmark located just northeast of the Old City features thousands of artifacts excavated during the British Mandate. Today it functions as part of the Israel Museum, also located in Jerusalem and considered to be one of the world's premier archaeology and art museums.

Headquarters of Zionist Executive,
King George Ave.,
1928–33
(ACC—New City)

> *People of Zion, who live in Jerusalem, you will weep no more.*
> *How gracious he will be when you cry for help!*
> *As soon as he hears, he will answer you."*
>
> Isaiah 30:19

The Jewish Agency

The Jewish Agency headquarters—formerly the Zionist Executive building—houses the government organization that helps Jews from the nations return home to the land of Israel.

Sultan's Pool

An ancient reservoir dating back to the first century BC, the Sultan's Pool was eventually
expanded and named by the Ottomans. Today it is located just outside the Old City's walls
and is a premier concert venue, gathering Jerusalem's multicultural residents.

> *No longer will they call you Deserted, or name your land Desolate. But you will be called
> Hephzibah, and your land Beulah; for the Lord will take delight in you, and your land will
> be married. As a young man marries a young woman, so will your Builder marry you."*

Isaiah 62:4-5

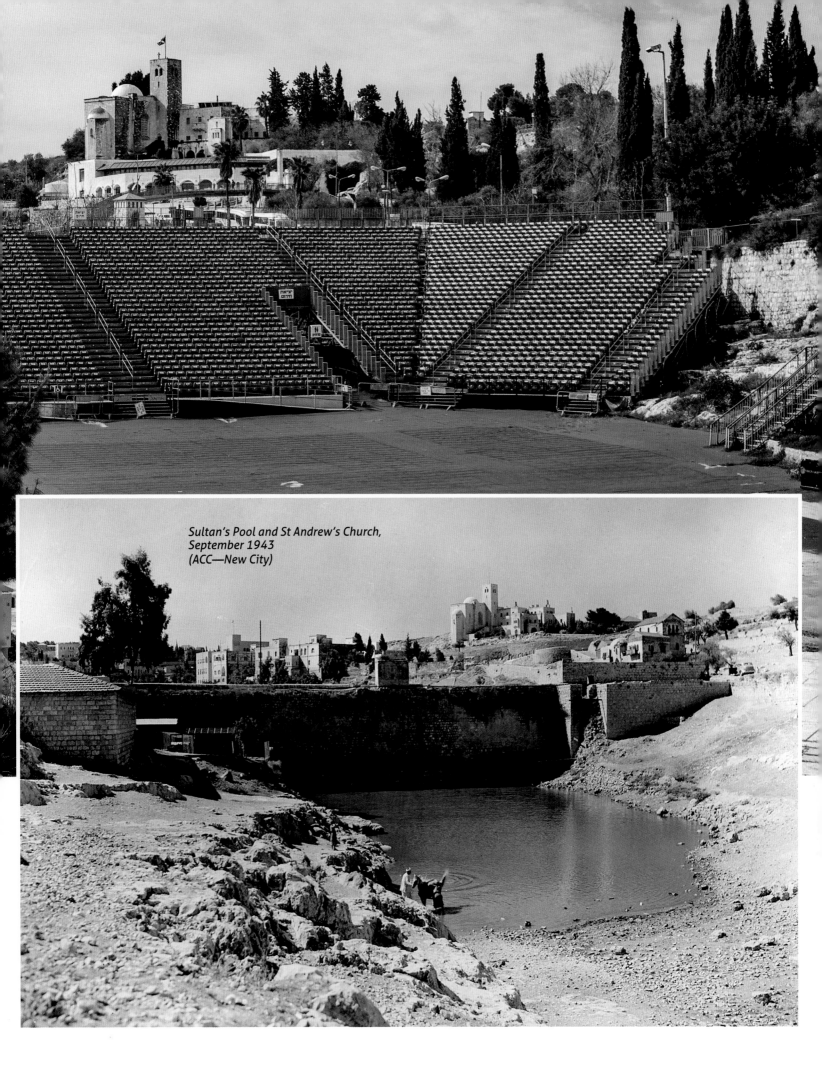

*Sultan's Pool and St Andrew's Church,
September 1943
(ACC—New City)*

*Mount of Olives,
1867
(Bergheim)*

*Mount of Olives,
1898–1914
(ACC—Mt. of Olives)*

Mount of Olives

In the center of these pictures is a small walled rectangle—the traditional site of the Garden of Gethsemane. Notice that in the 1867 photo, two significant churches are missing. The Russian Orthodox Church of Saint Mary Magdalene, with its prominent golden cupolas, was completed in 1888. The Roman Catholic Church of All Nations, also known as the Basilica of the Agony, was built directly to the right of the Garden. Finished in 1924, the church is easily recognizable by the blue domes on its roof.

> *'Pray for the peace of Jerusalem,'*
> *and thine own soul shall be refreshed."*
>
> *Charles Spurgeon, nineteenth-century Christian preacher and theologian,*
> *Evening by Evening* (New York: Sheldon, 1869), July 16

PANORAMAS of JERUSALEM

> " Beautiful in its loftiness, the joy of the whole earth, like the heights of Zaphon is Mount Zion, the city of the Great King."
>
> Psalm 48:2

View of Old City from Hebrew University on Mount Scopus

❝❝ *Our eyes felt that they could never grow weary of contemplating the Holy City.* ❞

Lady Judith Cohen Montefiore, 1839, British travel writer and philanthropist,

Notes from a Private Journal of a Visit to Egypt and Palestine (London: J. Rickerby, 1844), 274

Well at Ein-Rogel,
1857
(Frith)

“*These I will bring to my holy mountain and give them*
joy in my house of prayer. Their burnt offerings and
sacrifices will be accepted on my altar; for my house
will be called a house of prayer for all nations.”

Isaiah 56:7

Kidron Valley

A rare and seldom-seen view from the Kidron Valley floor, looking north toward the City of David and the Temple Mount. While not the most aesthetic photo, it captures the growth of the city over the last 160 years. This area and the well also have biblical significance as the location where David's friends Jonathan and Ahimaaz were hiding during Absalom's grab for David's throne (2 Samuel 17:17-21). Years later, David's son Adonijah staged his own coronation near this site in an attempt to steal the throne from his half brother Solomon (1 Kings 1:5-21).

City of David and Kidron Valley (Valley of Jehoshaphat), 1910–20 (ACC—City of David)

"'Jerusalem will be a city without walls because of the great number of people and animals in it. And I myself will be a wall of fire around it,' declares the LORD, 'and I will be its glory within.'"

Zechariah 2:4-5

Looking north up the Kidron Valley is like viewing three thousand years of history. On the left is the original City of David and the Temple Mount; on the right, the village of Silwan and the famed Mount of Olives. In the top center, the Hebrew University tower can be seen.

Kidron Valley (Valley of Jehoshaphat),
1858
(Frith)

❝ *During his lifetime Absalom had taken a pillar and erected it in the*
King's Valley as a monument to himself. . . . He named the pillar after
himself, and it is called Absalom's Monument to this day."

2 Samuel 18:18

> *Long before the word Zionism was uttered for the first time, old religious Jews came from all over the world to die in Jerusalem. It is the finest place to die in—it has always been acknowledged. It has a* joie de mourir *quite its own."*
>
> George Mikes, twentieth-century British journalist and humorist,
> *Coat of Many Colors: Israel* (Boston: Gambit, 1969), 102

*Silwan and Kidron Valley (Valley of Jehoshaphat),
1844
(Girault de Prangey)*

Village of Silwan

One of the oldest photos of Jerusalem ever taken, this view looks south toward a distant hillside and features the village of Silwan and the Kidron Valley in the foreground. Directly across the Kidron Valley lies the City of David, where David and the kings of Israel ruled (more on pages 36 and 96). Standing on the distant hillside provides a clear vista of all of Jerusalem and its surrounding valleys. Local guides have referred to it as the "Hill of Evil Counsel" since it was here that, in ancient times, a Roman garrison watched the city. In recent history, the British army built an outpost here that today is the United Nations building.

"Rejoice with Jerusalem and be glad for her,
all you who love her; rejoice greatly with
her, all you who mourn over her."

Isaiah 66:10

Mount Zion and Hinnom Valley,
1934–39
(ACC—Mount Zion)

" *Even in its present decay it is a beautiful city, and, if we [Jews]
come here, can become one of the most beautiful in the world again.* "

Theodor Herzl, October 29, 1898, Hungarian journalist and father of modern Zionism,
The Complete Diaries of Theodor Herzl, vol. 2 (New York: Herzl Press, 1960), 745

"You who bring good news to Jerusalem, lift up your voice with a shout, lift it up, do not be afraid; say to the towns of Judah, 'Here is your God!' See, the Sovereign LORD comes with power, and he rules with a mighty arm."

Isaiah 40:9-10

*Jerusalem from the South,
1898–1946
(ACC—Views of the City)*

Looking North

A view from Jerusalem's southern ridge, sometimes called the "Hill of
Evil Counsel" (see page 174). Today the Haas Promenade is here, a scenic
walking path that provides stunning views of the city and surrounding
valleys, making it a local favorite for picnics and events.

“ Let every Christian as much as in him lies engage himself
openly and publicly before all the World in some Mental
pursuit for the Building up of Jerusalem.”

William Blake, eighteenth-century poet,

quoted in *Jerusalem: The Emanation of the Giant Albion,*
ed. Morton D. Paley (Princeton, NJ: Princeton University Press, 1991), 258

View of the Old City from the Mount of Olives, Looking Northwest,
1898–1914
(ACC—Views of the City)

❝*This is the city so beloved by God.*❞

Francesco Suriano, sixteenth-century Venetian merchant and Franciscan guardian,
in *Treatise on the Holy Land*, 42, quoted in Jack Friedman, *The Jerusalem Book of Quotations*, 103

The people will play flutes and sing,
'The source of my life springs from Jerusalem!'"

Psalm 87:7, NLT

View of the Old City from the Mount of Olives, Looking West over the Kidron Valley, 1898–1910
(ACC—Views of the City)

> ❝ *As the mountains surround Jerusalem,*
> *so the L*ORD *surrounds his people both*
> *now and forevermore.*"
>
> Psalm 125:2

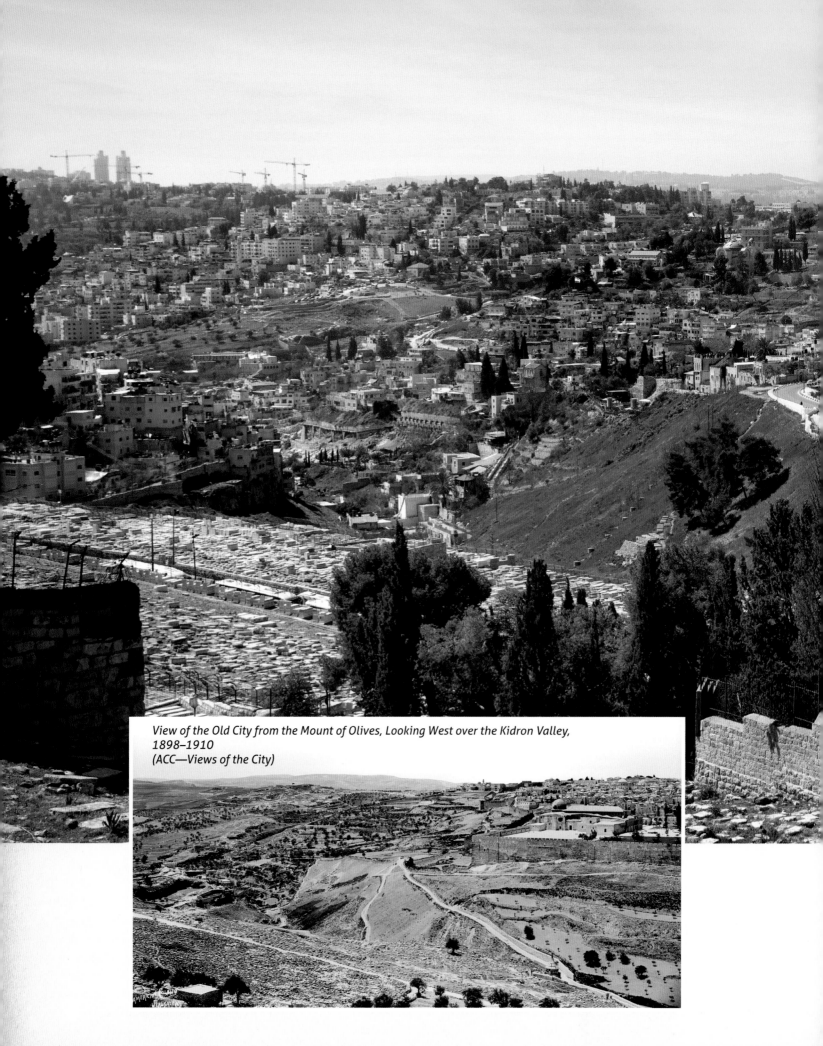

View of the Old City from the Mount of Olives, Looking West over the Kidron Valley, 1898–1910
(ACC—Views of the City)

“ *The view from the Mount of Olives is one which, from its strange beauty and its extraordinary interest, lingers long and lovingly in the memory of those who have seen it.*”

Sir Charles William Wilson, 1864, English explorer and researcher,

Picturesque Palestine, Sinai, and Egypt, 4

View of Jerusalem from Mount Scopus, 1844 (Girault de Prangey)

"If I forget you, Jerusalem, may my right hand forget its skill. May my tongue cling to the roof of my mouth if I do not remember you, if I do not consider Jerusalem my highest joy."

Psalm 137:5-6

Jerusalem from Mount Scopus,
1925–34
(ACC—Views of the City)

> *A fast walker could go outside the walls of Jerusalem and walk entirely around the city in an hour. I do not know how else to make one understand how small it is. The appearance of the city is peculiar. It is as knobby with countless little domes as a prison door is with bolt-heads.*"

Mark Twain, 1867,
The Innocents Abroad, 558

View from Mount Scopus

Mount Scopus, today home to Hebrew University, is one of the best vantage points for viewing the dramatic changes in Jerusalem over the last 175 years, when the population increased from 15,000 residents to nearly 1 million.

Old City Walls from the Southwest, Hebron Road,
1860
(Bergheim)

" *The Lᴏʀᴅ has chosen Zion, he has desired it for his*
dwelling, saying, 'This is my resting place for ever and
ever; here I will sit enthroned, for I have desired it.'"

Psalm 132:13-14

*Without Jerusalem, the land of Israel is as a body without a soul.**"*

Elhanan Leib Lewinsky, 1857–1910, Ukranian Hebrew writer and Zionist leader

"Jerusalem: Famous Quotations," jewishvirtuallibrary.org

" *I will make the lame my remnant, those driven away a strong nation.
The LORD will rule over them in Mount Zion from that day and forever. As
for you, watchtower of the flock, stronghold of Daughter Zion, the former
dominion will be restored to you; kingship will come to Daughter Jerusalem.*"

Micah 4:7-8

Looking Northwest

Standing above the village of Silwan, this view looks north and shows not only the excavation of the southern Temple steps but also the new buildings and life surrounding the Old City.

> *Many peoples will come and say, 'Come, let us go up to the mountain of the LORD, to the temple of the God of Jacob. He will teach us his ways, so that we may walk in his paths.' The law will go out from Zion, the word of the LORD from Jerusalem."*
>
> Isaiah 2:3

PERSONAL ENCOUNTERS
An Outpouring of Love and Support

During one of my frequent stays at a local guest house, I borrowed an item from my neighbor Tal. Upon my returning it with thanks, Tal, true to Israeli style, invited me in for coffee, which soon turned into a meal. Tal and her husband, Itzak, a fascinating Israeli couple in their late fifties, were looking forward to early retirement following many successful years of business in the United States and Israel.

After asking more about my books and my tour company, Ezra Adventures, Tal commented with usual Israeli directness, *"Wow, you are quite the Zionist. I'm not sure that would be something I would give my life to, but . . ."* Her sentence trailed off as she smiled and gave a casual shrug.

Undeterred, I offered her a look at my first photo book, *Israel Rising*, which I happened to have in my bag. Tal

turned the pages, viewing the then-now pictures from locations she'd known from childhood. Then she read one of the Personal Encounters stories. Enraptured, her demeanor changed as her hand went to her chest. *"Wow . . . this is so . . . oh, what's the word in English?"*

"Heart stirring?" I ventured.

"Yes!" Tal exclaimed with the surprise of the emotion she was feeling. She continued to thoughtfully page through the book. When Itzak returned home for lunch, Tal urged him to look at the before-and-after photos of his hometown. *"You need to see these pictures from Afula!"* she remarked.

Soon Itzak was immersed in our conversation about Israel's restoration, as if he had been present with us from the beginning. With wonder in his voice, he said, *"A few years ago, we were at a large event that [former Fox News talk show host and American conservative] Glenn Beck put on in Israel. We decided to go hear what he had to say. Most of the people at the conference were from other nations, and we were shocked at their outpouring of love for Israel! If three thousand Israelis had attended, we wouldn't have seen that type of love for Israel. We were so touched! I don't remember anything that was said that night, but I will never forget the love and support we felt. It was amazing."*

Although that event was years ago, Itzak spoke of it as if it were yesterday. Just a few generations ago, only a remnant of people thought about Jerusalem's restoration or even dreamed of Israel becoming a nation again. Today the hearts of people from all over the world are starting to return to Jerusalem and her people. And Israel is taking notice.

CONCLUSION
The City of Peace Reawakens

For the first time in almost two millennia, dramatic and unprecedented changes are happening in the city of Jerusalem. Perhaps what's most amazing is that many of them were foretold more than 2,500 years ago. Let's look again at aspects of this ancient prophecy from Zechariah 8:4-8:

This is what the Lord Almighty says: "Once again men and women of ripe old age will sit in the streets of Jerusalem, each of them with cane in hand because of their age. The city streets will be filled with boys and girls playing there."

This is what the Lord Almighty says: "It may seem marvelous to the remnant of this people at that time, but will it seem marvelous to me?" declares the

Lord Almighty.

This is what the Lord Almighty says: "I will save my people from the countries of the east and the west. I will bring them back to live in Jerusalem; they will be my people, and I will be faithful and righteous to them as their God."

We've already seen that until the Six-Day War in 1967, when Israel took full ownership of Jerusalem for the first time in more than two thousand years, the prophecies described above had not come to pass. Over the past fifty years, we've seen that despite occasional periods of unrest, peace and security have increasingly become a hallmark of life in Jerusalem. As history shows, this has not always been the norm.

Today, in the view of history, peace and security are growing in Jerusalem as never before. Just as prophesied in Zechariah 8:4-8, old men and women are walking in the streets with their canes, and children are playing there. God's people are returning to live in Jerusalem.

God also said through Zechariah that he would save his people from the nations to the east and to the west. The last one hundred years marks the first time in history that the Jewish people have been returning from nations all over the world. And they are coming back to Jerusalem. For centuries, travelers and locals alike commented on the dwindling population of Jerusalem and how quiet and forlorn the city was. According to a 1906 travel guide to Palestine, the population of Jerusalem was at least 60,000 people, with 40,000 of those Jews (Karl Baedeker, *Palestine and Syria Handbook for Travellers*, 4th ed. [New York: Charles Scribner's Sons, 1906], 22, 24). In 111 years, the population multiplied many times over to 559,800 Jews out of a total population of 901,300 in 2017 (Peggy Cidor, "The Holy City: Jerusalem by the Numbers," *Jerusalem Post*, May 21, 2020, jpost.com).

Now let's consider Zechariah 8:12:

The seed will grow well, the vine will yield its fruit, the ground will produce its crops, and the heavens will drop their dew. I will give all these things as an inheritance to the remnant of this people.

It's happening right now: The physical land has responded to the presence and care of the Jewish people in Jerusalem, who have cultivated it and are bound to it by an everlasting covenant. In the last one hundred years, after a decimating four-hundred-year period of Ottoman rule, the Jewish National Fund has replanted entire forests around Jerusalem, bringing big changes to the city and its surrounding areas. Weather patterns have brought more dew and rain, topsoil is being naturally re-created, and animal populations are returning. While the city had begun growing prior to the rebirth of the nation in 1948, it had not experienced

anything close to this type of growth and production since the Hasmonean Kingdom before the time of the Romans (142–63 BC). Today it is flourishing like never before as exports of flowers, fruits, and vegetables grown on farms surrounding Jerusalem are being shipped around the world. And after centuries of travelers and locals alike commenting on the dwindling population of Jerusalem and how quiet and forlorn the city was, the nations are now streaming to Israel, and specifically Jerusalem:

This is what the LORD Almighty says: "Many peoples and the inhabitants of many cities will yet come, and the inhabitants of one city will go to another and say, 'Let us go at once to entreat the LORD and seek the LORD Almighty. I myself am going.' And many peoples and powerful nations will come to Jerusalem to seek the LORD Almighty and to entreat him."

This is what the LORD Almighty says: "In those days ten people from all languages and nations will take firm hold of one Jew by the hem of his robe and say, 'Let us go with you, because we have heard that God is with you.'"

ZECHARIAH 8:20-23

The year 2019 was a record for tourism in Israel, surpassing the 4.5-million-visitors mark for the first time ever (Eytan Halon, "Israel Welcomes Record-Breaking 4.55 Million Tourists in 2019," *Jerusalem Post*, December 29, 2019, jpost.com), and according to statistics from 2016, it's likely that at least 78 percent of these visitors also went to Jerusalem (see "Jerusalem Is Moving in the Right Direction: Statistics and Numbers," Israel Ministry of Foreign Affairs, mfa.gov.il). Regardless of their purpose for coming, never before in history have the nations shown such interest in seeing Israel and visiting its capital city, Jerusalem.

Perhaps even more stunning is that amid the rise of anti-Semitism around the world, an unprecedented rise in support for the Jewish people has come from the nations, primarily from Christians within those nations. While it is difficult to find a 100-year time span in the last 1,700 years when a segment of the Christian church has not been directly or indirectly involved in the persecution of the Jewish people, the tide is beginning to turn. Organizations with millions of members, such as Christians United for Israel, are becoming vocal defenders and active advocates for Israel and the Jewish people.

Both the government of Israel and the religious Jewish community are taking notice. Israeli Prime Minister Benjamin Netanyahu has been quoted several times saying that Christians are Israel's best friends, and in 2015, a group of Orthodox rabbis from Israel, Europe, and the US made a public statement calling Christianity part of God's divine plan and a gift to the nations. Both declarations would have seemed far-fetched or impossible only thirty years ago, yet today these relationships are beginning to change in a way the world has never seen—and exactly as the prophets foretold.

If these examples from Zechariah 8 are coming to pass in practical and tangible ways, what should we make of the first part of the prophecy?

This is what the LORD says: "I will return to Zion and dwell in Jerusalem. Then Jerusalem will be called the Faithful City, and the mountain of the LORD Almighty will be called the Holy Mountain."
ZECHARIAH 8:3

I don't pretend to have an explanation for why this verse precedes the others we've looked at. But I do know that the other portions of this ancient prophecy, which at one time seemed utterly idealistic, are unfolding in tangible detail for the first time ever. Perhaps we should expect more of the same practical fulfillments, whether we can see them clearly now or not.

One thing is for certain: An increasing number of Jews and Christians are seeing them as a sign and are awaiting the Lord's arrival in Jerusalem. I have a friend who has witnessed the massive increase in tourism and crowd congestion while living in Jerusalem's Old City for the last twenty years. He has wryly joked, *"When the Messiah is ruling in Jerusalem and all nations are coming to worship here, I hope he has a better traffic plan."* Yes, I'm sure he has thought of that as well.

In our day, Jerusalem, the City of Peace, is reawakening.

> *Awake, awake, Zion, clothe yourself with strength!*
> *Put on your garments of splendor, Jerusalem, the holy city. . . .*
> *Shake off your dust; rise up, sit enthroned, Jerusalem."*
>
> Isaiah 52:1-2

HISTORICAL REFERENCES
The Hearts of Men

Through the millennia, people from multiple empires, backgrounds, and faiths have felt the inexplicable magnetism of Jerusalem, more so than toward any other city in the world. The lure on their hearts is undeniable. Whether from good or evil motivations, the following quotes represent a small cross section of those responses over the last two thousand years.

First Century

"The rest of Judaea is divided into ten Local Government Areas . . . [including] the district that formally contained Jerusalem, by far the most famous city of the East and not of Judaea only." —*Pliny the Elder, AD 23–79, Roman naturalist* (Natural History, *vol. 2 [Cambridge, MA: Harvard University Press, 1989], 273, 275)*

"The Romans, although they were greatly distressed in getting together their materials, raised their banks in one and twenty days, after they had cut down all the trees that were in the country that adjoined to the city, and that for ninety furlongs [eleven miles] round about [Jerusalem]. . . . And truly, the very view itself was a melancholy thing; for those places which were before adorned with trees and pleasant gardens, were now become a desolate country every way, and its trees were all cut down: nor could any foreigner that had formerly seen Judea and the most beautiful suburbs of the city, and now saw it as a desert, but lament and mourn sadly at so great a change; for the war had laid all the signs of beauty quite waste; nor if any one that had known the place before, had come on a sudden to it now, would he have known it again; but though he were at the city itself, yet would he have inquired for it notwithstanding." —*Flavius Josephus, AD 37–100, first-century Jewish-Roman historian* (The Wars of the Jews, *272)*

Second Century

"I and others, who are right-minded Christians on all points, are assured that there will be a resurrection of the dead, and a thousand years in Jerusalem, which will then be built, adorned, and enlarged, [as] the prophets Ezekiel and Isaiah and others declare." —Justin Martyr, AD 100–165, *early Christian church father and apologist* (The Writings of Justin Martyr and Athenagoras *[Edinburgh: T & T Clark, 1892], 200)*

"Jews . . . are distinguished from the rest of mankind in practically every detail of life, and especially by the fact that they do not honour any of the usual gods, but show extreme reverence for one particular divinity. They never had any statue of him even in Jerusalem itself, but believing him to be unnamable and invisible, they worship him in the most extravagant fashion on earth. They built to him a temple." —Dio Cassius, AD 155–235, *Roman statesman and historian (T. E. Page and W. H. D. Rouse, eds.,* Dio's Roman History, *vol. 3, trans. Earnest Carey [London: William Heinemann, 1914], 127)*

Fourth Century

"As Judaea is exalted above all other provinces, so is this city [Jerusalem] exalted above all Judaea." —Saint Jerome, AD 347–420, *author of the Vulgate translation of the Bible (Letter 46, "Paula and Eustochium to Marcella," in* The Principal Works of St. Jerome, *trans. W. H. Fremantle, et al., A Select Library of Nicene and Post-Nicene Fathers of the Christian Church, vol. 6 [New York: The Christian Literature Company, 1893], 61)*

Fifth Century

"No other sentiment draws people to Jerusalem than the desire to see and touch the places where Christ was physically present, and to be able to say from their very own experience, 'We have worshipped in the places where his feet have stood.'" —Paulinus of Nola, AD 353–431, *Roman poet and senator (Epistle 49:14, in Hoyland and Williamson, eds.,* The Oxford Illustrated History of the Holy Land *[Oxford, UK: Oxford University Press, 2018], 293)*

Sixth Century

"A bride that was in Jerusalem did not need to adorn herself with perfumes, since she was perfumed by the fragrance of the incense, which filled the air of Jerusalem." (Talmud, Yoma 39b, sefaria.org)

"One who did not see Jerusalem in its glory, never saw a beautiful city. One who did not see the Temple in its constructed state, never saw a magnificent structure." (Talmud, Sukkah 51b, sefaria.org)

"Ten [measures] of beauty descended to the world; Jerusalem took nine and all the rest of the world in its entirety took one." (Talmud, Kiddushin 49b, sefaria.org)

"Even at the time of Jerusalem's failure, trustworthy people did not cease [from living] there." (Talmud, Shabbat, 119b, sefaria.org)

"'A city, the fame of which has gone out from one end of the world to the other.' . . . This—explains the Talmud—'is Jerusalem.'" (quoted in Alfred Edersheim, Sketches of Jewish Social Life in the Time of Christ [Boston: Ira Bradley & Co., 1881], 82)

Seventh Century

"A sin committed at Jerusalem is the equivalent of a thousand sins, and a good work there is the equal to a thousand good works." —"A Tradition of Muhammed," AD 570–632 (F. E. Peters, Jerusalem: The Holy City in the Eyes of Chroniclers, Visitors, Pilgrims, and Prophets from the Days of Abraham to the Beginnings of Modern Times [Princeton, New Jersey: Princeton University Press, 2017], 379)

"In his sermon on Christmas Day 634, the patriarch of Jerusalem, Sophronius, lamented over the impossibility of going on pilgrimage to Bethlehem as was the custom, because the Christians were being forcibly kept in Jerusalem: 'not detained by tangible bonds, but chained and nailed by fear of the Saracens,' whose 'savage, barbarous and bloody sword' kept them locked up in the town." (quoted in Bat Ye'or, The Decline of Eastern Christianity under Islam [Madison, NJ: Fairleigh Dickinson University Press, 1996], 44)

Ninth Century

"The land of Israel sits in the middle of the world, and Jerusalem in the middle of the land of Israel, and the Temple in the middle of Jerusalem, and the palace [Holy of Holies] in the middle of the Temple, and the ark in the middle of the palace and the Foundation stone before the palace from which the world was founded." (Midrash Tanchuma, Kedoshim, Siman 10, sefaria.org)

Tenth Century

"Anyone who prays in Jerusalem is as if they pray before the Throne of Glory, because the gate of heaven is there." (Midrash Tehillim, 91:5, sefaria.org)

"Jerusalem is the most illustrious of cities. . . . Still Jerusalem has some disadvantages. Thus, it is reported as found written in the Torah, that 'Jerusalem is a golden basin filled with scorpions.'" —Mukaddasi, AD 946–1000, Muslim historian, geographer, and native of Jerusalem (Description of Syria, Including Palestine, trans. Guy Le Strange [London: Palestine Pilgrims' Text Society, 1886], 36–37)

Eleventh Century

"Spain is my country and Jerusalem, my destiny."— Judah Halevi, 1075–1141, Jewish scholar and poet (Letter quoted in Mordechai Naor, City of Hope [Ra'anana, Israel: Chemed Books, 1996], 137)

"Christians, hasten to help your brothers in the East, for they are being attacked. Arm for the rescue of

Jerusalem under your captain Christ. Wear his cross as your badge. If you are killed your sins will be pardoned." —Pope Urban II in 1095 (Michael Wenkart, 50 Events in the History of Mankind [Norderstedt, Germany: Books on Demand, 2014], 110)

Twelfth Century

"O what their joy and their glory must be, those endless sabbaths the blessed ones see; crown for the valiant, to weary ones rest; God shall be all, and in all ever blest. Truly, 'Jerusalem' name we that shore, city of peace that brings joy evermore; wish and fulfillment are not severed there, nor do things prayed for come short of the prayer." —Peter Abelard, 1079–1142, French theologian, philosopher, and logician ("Oh, What Their Joy and Their Glory Must Be," trans. John Mason Neale, in The Church Hymnal, revised, ed. Charles L. Hutchins [Boston: The Parish Choir, 1920], 367)

Thirteenth Century

"Great is the solitude and great the devastation. . . . Jerusalem is more desolate than the rest of the country . . . but even in this destruction it is a blessed land." —Nachmanides (Rabbi Moshe ben Nachman), Spanish rabbi and Talmudic scholar, in a letter to his son in 1267, (quoted in Franz Kobler, ed., Letters of Jews through the Ages, vol. 1 [New York: East and West Library/The Jewish Publication Society, 1978], 226)

Fourteenth Century

"Lo! the most holy, the most royal, and most noble, and magnificent above all the cities of the world, you, Jerusalem." —Niccolò of Poggibonsi, Italian Franciscan, a pilgrim to the Holy Land from 1346–50 (A Voyage beyond the Seas [Jerusalem: Franciscan Press, 1945], 9)

"Jesu in mercy send me wit to guide your way one further stage upon that perfect, glorious pilgrimage called the celestial, to Jerusalem." —Geoffrey Chaucer, 1343–1400, father of English literature ("The Parson's Prologue," The Canterbury Tales, trans. Nevill Coghill [New York: Penguin Books, 2003], 486)

Fifteenth Century

"When I saw [Jerusalem's] ruins I rent my garments a hand breadth, and in the bitterness of my heart recited the appropriate prayer." —Rabbi Meshullam ben Rabbi Menahem of Volterra, 1481 (Jewish Travellers in the Middle Ages: 19 Firsthand Accounts, ed. Elkan Nathan Adler [New York: Dover, 1987], 189)

"I propose to your Majesties that all the profit to be derived from my enterprise should be used for the recovery of Jerusalem." —Christopher Columbus, AD 1451–1506, Italian explorer and navigator (Joshua Prawer, The World of the Crusaders [New York: Quadrangle, 1973], 152)

Sixteenth Century

"*The picture. A great plain, comprising the entire Jerusalem district, where is the supreme Commander-in-Chief of the forces of good, Christ our Lord: another plain near Babylon, where Lucifer is, at the head of the enemy.*" —*Saint Ignatius of Loyola, 1491–1556, Spanish Catholic priest* (The Spiritual Exercises of Saint Ignatius of Loyola, *trans. Thomas Corbishley [Mineola, NY: Dover, 1963], fourth day: 138, 52*)

"*So part we sadly in this troublous world to meet with joy in sweet Jerusalem.*" —*William Shakespeare, 1564–1616* (Henry VI, Part III, *ed. William Montgomery [New York: Penguin Books, 2000], 122*)

Eighteenth Century

"*The [Hebrew] word [kotel = Western Wall] is to be divided into two words:* ko *which has the same numerical value as God's name [26] and* tel *which means 'the hill' towards which all turn and direct their prayers.*" —*Moses Yerushalmi, Karaite pilgrim, in 1769 (Yaari,* Masa'ot Eretz Yisrael, *449, quoted in Jack Friedman,* The Jerusalem Book of Quotations, *134*)

Nineteenth Century

"*[Jerusalem] is a city shining in light and color! . . . The view is the most splendid that can be presented to the eye of a city that is no more.*" —*Alphonse de Lamartine, French poet, novelist, and statesman, October 28, 1837 (*Souvenirs, Impressions, Pensées et Paysages pendant un Voyage en Orient, *quoted in* Famous Travellers to the Holy Land, *comp. Linda Osband [Miami: Parkwest, 1991], 70–71)*

"*Were I asked what was the object of the greatest interest that I had seen, and the scene that made the deepest impression upon me . . . I would say that it was a Jew mourning over the stones of Jerusalem.*" —*William Robert Wilde, 1815–76, surgeon and writer (Osband,* Famous Travellers to the Holy Land, *155)*

"*Jerusalem . . . the theater of the most memorable and stupendous events that have ever occurred in the annals of the world.*" —*J. T. Barclay, American physician and missionary, 1858* (The City of the Great King *[Ann Arbor, MI: University of Michigan Library, 2006], xii)*

"*Of all cities in the world, [Jerusalem] has the distinction of being the battle-ground for religious creeds—the field where the fanaticism of the Jew, the Christian, and the Turk has met, and alternately triumphed.*" —*W. H. Bartlett, English artist, author, and traveler, 1863* (Jerusalem Revisited *[London: Thomas Nelson & Sons, 1863], 192)*

"*There is no place I so much desire to see as Jerusalem.*" —*US President Abraham Lincoln, April 14, 1865, his last words to Mrs. Lincoln before his assassination* (Stephen Mansfield, Lincoln's Battle with God: A President's Struggle with Faith and What It Meant for America *[Nashville: Thomas Nelson, 2012], xvii)*

Twentieth Century

"*Nowhere else has this universal struggle [between the spirit of God and the spirit of man] been waged so consciously, so articulately as in Jerusalem.*" —*George Adam Smith, Scottish theologian, 1907* (Jerusalem: The Topography, Economics and History from the Earliest Times to A.D. 70, *vol. 1 [London: Hodder and Stoughton, 1907], 5)*

"*It seems to me that it is entirely proper to start a Zionist State around Jerusalem.*" —*US President Theodore Roosevelt, 1918 (Michael B. Oren,* Power, Faith, and Fantasy: America in the Middle East: 1776 to the Present *[New York: W. W. Norton, 2007], 359)*

"*Rabbi Abraham Isaac Kook, a former chief rabbi of the Holy Land [first rabbi of the British Mandate of Palestine, 1921–35, and a father of religious Zionism], once said: 'There are men with hearts of stone and there are stones with human hearts.' He was referring to the stones of the Western Wall.*" *(Meir Ben-Dov, et al.,* Western Wall (HaKotel) *[Israel: Ministry of Defence, 1984], 36–37)*

"*The United Nations saw fit this year to decide that our eternal city should become a corpus separatum under international control. Our rebuttal of this wicked counsel was unequivocal and resolute: The Government and Knesset at once moved their seat to Jerusalem and made Israel's crown and capital irrevocable and for all men to see.*" —*David Ben-Gurion, Israel's first prime minister, 1949 (John W.*

Wohlfarth, Elysium [AuthorHouse, 2001], 388)

"Perhaps in this as in other critical periods of history a free Jerusalem may proclaim redemption to mankind." —Abba Eban, Israeli diplomat, 1957 (Voice of Israel [London: Faber & Faber, 1957], 61)

"After all my possessions had been burned, God gave me the wisdom to return to Jerusalem." —Shmuel Yosef Agnon, Nobel Prize Laureate writer, 1966 ("Shmuel Agnon Banquet Speech," nobelprize.org)

"The tears here [Jerusalem] do not soften the eyes. They only hone and polish the hard face, like a rock."

—Yehuda Amichai, Israeli poet, 1971 ("Jerusalem's Suicide Attempts," trans. Benjamin and Barbara Harshav, in The Poetry of Yehuda Amichai, ed. Robert Alter [New York: Farrar, Straus and Giroux, 2015], 178)

"I, too, feel that the light of Jerusalem has purifying powers and filters the blood and the thoughts; I don't forbid myself the reflection that light may be the outer garment of God." —Saul Bellow, Jewish-American novelist, 1976 (To Jerusalem and Back: A Personal Account [New York: Penguin Books, 1998], 93)

"This beautiful golden city is the heart and soul of the Jewish people. You cannot live without a heart and soul. If you want one simple word to symbolize all of Jewish history, that word would be Jerusalem." —Teddy Kollek, mayor of Jerusalem from 1965–93 ("Jerusalem," Foreign Affairs, July 1977)

"A phone call from Jerusalem to Heaven is a local call, not charged as long distance." —attributed to Menachem Begin, Israeli prime minister from

1977–83 (Eliyahu Tal, Whose Jerusalem? [Israel: International Forum for a United Jerusalem, 1994], 15)

"Jerusalem is a festival and a lamentation. Its song is a sigh across the ages, a delicate, robust, mournful psalm at the great junction of spiritual cultures."

—David K. Shipler, Pulitzer Prize–winning author, 1986 (Arab and Jew: Wounded Spirits in a Promised Land, rev. ed. [New York: Broadway Books, 2015], 1)

"[Yasser Arafat] called for 'martyrs by the millions' to rise for the Palestinian cause." —Judith Miller quoting Yasser Arafat, 1929–2004, former chairman of the Palestine Liberation Organization and known terrorist ("Yasir Arafat, Father and Leader of Palestinian Nationalism, Dies at 75," New York Times, November 11, 2004, nytimes.com)

"Sir, I salute your courage, your strength, your indefatigability. And I want you to know that we are with you until victory, until victory, until Jerusalem." —George Galloway, former member of the British Parliament, in a speech to Iraqi dictator Saddam Hussein (Quoted from the London Times, January 20, 1994, in "Why the Media Are Critical of Galloway," The Guardian, May 14, 2005, theguardian.com)

Twenty-First Century

"To open the Bible is to open a window toward Jerusalem, as Daniel did . . . no matter where our exile may have taken us." —N. T. Wright, New Testament scholar and Anglican bishop (After You Believe: Why Christian Character Matters [New York: HarperCollins, 2012], 261)

"It is more than twenty years since we both left the city. This is a serious chunk of time, longer than the years we spent living there. Yet we still think of Jerusalem as our home. Not home in the sense of the place you conduct your daily life or constantly return to. In fact, Jerusalem is our home almost against our wills. It is our home because it defines us, whether we like it or not." —Yotam Ottolenghi, Israeli-English chef and culinary writer (Jerusalem: A Cookbook [Berkeley, CA: Ten Speed Press, 2012], 9)

"We promise you that we will not cede a single part of Palestine, we will not cede Jerusalem, we will continue to fight and we will not lay down our arms." —Ismail Haniyeh, leader of the terrorist group Hamas (Elad Benari, "Haniyeh Promises 'Difficult Days' for Israel," Arutz Sheva 7, January 9, 2012, israelnationalnews.com)

"That's where peace begins—not just in the plans of leaders, but in the hearts of people. Not just in some carefully designed process, but in the daily connections—that sense of empathy that takes place among those who live together in this land and in this sacred city of Jerusalem." —US President Barack Obama, March 21, 2013 ("Remarks of President Barack Obama to the People of Israel," The White House: President Barack Obama, obamawhitehouse.archives.gov)

"Palestinian President Mahmoud Abbas called on the entire Palestinian population to form an army and march on Jerusalem. Abbas added that 'millions of fighters, along with the Arab, Islamic, and Christian nations will march against Jerusalem.'" —David Lazarus quoting Palestinian president Mahmoud Abbas ("Palestinian President Calls for a Million Martyrs to March on Jerusalem," Israel Today, August 23, 2019, israeltoday.co.il)

"In this city that we had to leave in tears during the First World War, it is still possible to come across traces of the Ottoman resistance. So Jerusalem is our city, a city from us." —Recep Tayyip Erdoğan, president of Turkey, addressing Turkish lawmakers (quoted in Raphael Ahren, "'Jerusalem Is Our City,' Turkey's Erdogan Declares," The Times of Israel, October 1, 2020, timesofisrael.com)

"In 1995, Congress adopted the Jerusalem Embassy Act, urging the federal government to relocate the American embassy to Jerusalem and to recognize that that city—and so importantly—is Israel's capital. . . . Yet, for over 20 years, every previous American president has exercised the law's waiver, refusing to move the U.S. embassy to Jerusalem or to recognize Jerusalem as Israel's capital city. . . . Therefore, I have determined that it is time to officially recognize Jerusalem as the capital of Israel. . . . Through all of these years, presidents representing the United States have declined to officially recognize Jerusalem as Israel's capital. In fact, we have declined to acknowledge any Israeli capital at all. But today, we finally acknowledge the obvious: that Jerusalem is Israel's capital. This is nothing more, or less, than a recognition of reality. It is also the right thing to do. It's something that has to be done." —US President Donald Trump, December 6, 2017 ("Statement by President Trump on Jerusalem," trumpwhitehouse.archives.gov)